Dear Mik

Dear Tom

God's Faithfulness in

Every Season of Grief

Trust Him —
He is the faithful
God! _Deut 7:9_

D A N A   H O B B S

Dana
_10/28/2019_

ISBN 978-1-64299-435-3 (paperback)
ISBN 978-1-64299-436-0 (digital)

Christian Faith Publishing, Inc.
832 Park Avenue
Meadville, PA 16335
www.christianfaithpublishing.com

All scripture references are from the New International Version (NIV) unless otherwise noted.

Printed in the United States of America

To April, Ali, Amy, and Andrew

The gift of being your Mom is the fulfillment of all I have ever wanted to be. You are my heart and soul. "Blessed is she who has believed that the Lord would fulfill his promises to her" (Luke 1:45)

This will be written for the generation to come, that
a people yet to be created may praise the LORD.

—Psalm 102:18

Introduction

In July 2009, I began writing letters to my husband through an online blog format. This started out as a convenient way to keep our family and friends updated on his declining health. Seven months later, writing letters to him became a way for me to process his death. Although many people gently recommended that I see a therapist or suggested that maybe my physician should prescribe medication for depression, I chose to write. For six months after his death I shared my letters publicly then decided it was time to write them privately. Recording the good, bad, and often the very raw and ugly, yet oddly beautiful, journey through grief.

Because, make no mistake about it, we will each be faced with grief at some point. We may have different experiences and different coping mechanisms, but grief is a journey we must all eventually travel *through*. We cannot go over it, under it, or around it. Grief is not something we run away from for very long. Grief will come to each of us in many different forms. Whether through death, divorce, fractured relationships with our children, financial devastation, or shattered dreams.

Because the journey through grief is one we will all travel, it is up to each of us to decide whether grief will define us or refine us—whether grief will become our way of life or a season of our life.

This is my personal journey through the season of grief . . .

For Trish and Jenny:

I first met Trish when we were students at Whitesburg Jr High in Huntsville, Alabama. After we graduated from Grissom High School in 1979, life took us in separate directions. We would each go on to marry the love of our life, raise our children, and have careers. In the summer of 2012 Trish's husband, Gary was diagnosed with cancer and the prognosis was not good. Knowing that Tom had died, she contacted me and we began communicating regularly. Through deep sadness, our friendship was renewed. Three months later Gary died.

I met Jenny in 2014. Each of us had recently moved to Houston, and we ended up working at the same office. Although there is a thirty-year age difference, Jenny and I became fast friends. Our shared hometown and common circle of friends became a bond for us. Jenny's boyfriend, Clint, was also from Huntsville and was working in Houston as well. About a year after Jenny and I met, Clint was diagnosed with a rare form of cancer, and Jenny became his primary caregiver during his treatments. When Clint died in July 2017, he and Jenny had been married for eighty-five days.

Trish and Jenny, watching each of you walk the different roads that lead you to this place in life has been such a ministry to me and those who are blessed to know you. You each possess a sweet, graceful spirit and brave determination that inspires me to be a better person. I pray that on the following pages, you find words of encouragement from someone who is just a few steps ahead of you in the season of grief. Someone who has learned firsthand that Isaiah 61:3 is true. God will bring "beauty from ashes, joy from mourning, and strength from despair."

Trust Him, He will not fail you.

"And I remain confident of this: I will see the goodness of the Lord in the land of the living" (Psalm 27:13).

Texas or Bust

July 6, 2014

It's two thirty in the morning and I can't sleep. I'm vacillating between mind-numbing excitement and sheer terror. Parked in my parent's driveway in Holly Pond, Alabama, is the biggest U-Haul I've ever seen, and it's stuffed to the gills with almost all my worldly possessions. In a few hours, our oldest child and I will pull out of the driveway and head to Houston to start my new adventure.

And although this decision has been bathed . . . drenched . . . in prayer, I am now sitting in the dark, wondering if I have lost my mind.

How did I get to this moment? What will happen if I change my mind?

Regardless of the peace I felt just hours ago, my heart is fearful. I've never lived alone, and the thought of possibly being alone for the rest of my life is paralyzing. I've never been totally responsible for my financial well-being. Can I make it on my own? Have I done the math correctly, or am I about to board a ship that is doomed to sink?

So many people have told me that you would be proud of my adventurous spirit. I hope you would be. But right now, I believe this is either the wisest and bravest thing I have ever done, or quite possibly I am about to make the dumbest mistake of my life.

How We Got Here

Today was the end of our life as we knew it. The black cloud has finally caught us. We've tried everything we can. Seen countless doctors and specialists. Tried every new drug as it was approved. But to no avail.

I remember so very well thirty-five years ago, coming to see you when you were home from school on bed rest. I thought how cool it was that you had a home tutor. You could watch *The Price is Right* while the rest of our friends from church were in English and Algebra II. We were eating school lunchroom food while your Daddy was bringing you Arby's. Friday nights we would come over and watch TV in your den. I had no idea just how sick you were. I only knew that you were on bed rest, and thanks to your tutor you were making great grades. I was freakishly jealous.

When we married in 1980, I understood that you had a kidney disease and that sometime in the future you would face the possibility of dialysis and a transplant; but that was in the future. We were so young. You seemed so healthy. We had our dreamy storybook life to live.

And now twenty-nine years later, we find ourselves dealing with the black cloud we have been running from for so long. Our hope was that we had a few more years before we had to take drastic measures. But last week, your kidneys ran out of steam. *End stage renal failure.* No real way to sugar coat it. No real way to outrun this runaway train.

As we face this new adventure in our lives, I think we are both realizing with a sober awareness that our empty nest years are not going to be as planned. And I cannot help but wonder, when have any of our plans ever worked in accordance with God's plan for our lives? As frightened and unsure of everything as I am right now, this I know . . . He is a good and perfect Savior. We are in His hands, and He will not fail us. We can trust Him.

It sounds so very simple . . . maybe because it is.

Sweet Fragrance

When I woke up this morning, I thought I smelled something familiar. I closed my eyes, and for some reason I was reminded of when we had the farm and would take the children and the four-wheeler and let them ride it through the trees on those trails. It was just a dirt road, but they thought it was a trail. For a moment, I could almost smell the honeysuckle. Remember how it would grow in the middle of the briers and thick brush? But the sweet honeysuckle smell was there.

This memory painted a picture for me that during pain, we can find the sweet fragrance of Christ. It's all around us. In the faces of our children and the words of encouragement from our friends, the faithful prayers lifted by our parents before we have opened our eyes each day, the message we hear delivered every Sunday at our church—these are a sweet fragrance of our Savior. Doesn't it smell wonderful?

I hope you can feel the prayers of those who love you so much. Those who hope with all they have that these treatments will make you feel better and prolong your life. I can't wait to see you when you get home this afternoon.

An Anxious Spirit

The first week of dialysis went as best as we could expect. No major issues, but after you did so great yesterday we were both disheartened to see that your feet were very swollen. I know you are disappointed, maybe even discouraged by this development. Everything seemed so good just a few hours earlier. I guess we should just know that it will take some time to get into a rhythm with this thing.

I must admit that for several days now I have been falling back into my old habit of questioning God again. I have tried to wear a happy face, but my spirit has been so anxious. Questions have overwhelmed the deepest part of my being . . . Why you? Why us? Why now? Why ever? How can we do this "thing" that has taken over our lives? How can we change this thing so that it doesn't take over our lives?

Matthew 6:34 tells me, "So do not worry about tomorrow; for tomorrow, will care for itself. Each day has enough trouble of its own."

In Exodus 16, Moses was leading the Israelites through the desert after escaping slavery in Egypt. In the margin of my Bible, I have written words I heard John Piper speak in a sermon. "Part of saving faith is the assurance that you will have faith tomorrow. Trusting Christ today includes trusting him to give you tomorrow's trust when tomorrow comes."

When his children were wandering in the wilderness, God could have provided a storehouse of provision for them at any moment. But he provided daily what they needed. Never more or less than the need. They had no place to store up for tomorrow, any excess would have been wasted. God was teaching the Israelites, and now you and I, that we must depend on his mercy. We will never receive today what we need for tomorrow, next week, or next year. Only what we need for the present moment we are in. But through this, he is teaching us to trust that our tomorrows, whatever they may bring, are in his hands. His character is only ever faithful and true.

When my anxious spirit begins to overwhelm me . . . and I start to doubt God's love for me or His ability to provide what I need, I am trying to remind my unbelieving heart of the words in Matthew 6 . . . to not be anxious about tomorrow, but to let tomorrow be anxious for itself. That Christ's compassions are new every morning. He is a faithful God. We can trust His heart.

Lotion

In Luke 7 beginning with verse 36, we read the story of a woman who has lived her life in sin. This woman, realizing that Jesus was in the same house as she, covered his feet with her tears and wiped them with her hair. She then used her most valued treasure, her alabaster perfume, and poured it on his feet. She did so with no regard to what those around her would think. She was just so thankful to be in the presence of the Savior. She recognized what an awesome moment she had before her.

Several days ago, you brought home a pamphlet that talked about how proper foot care is essential for dialysis patients. It explained how your feet will be the place where we will notice swelling the most and how you should keep them elevated when you are at home, that you should moisturize them daily.

When my grandparents were needing assistance at home and their children were staying with them, Mom used to rub Granddaddy's feet with lotion. She said this was one of her favorite things to do. It forced him to sit in his big chair by the front door . . . remember that old chair? They would turn off the TV and just talk. Or not. But it was their time to be together. The rest of the world would go by while they had that few moments each night. Just the briefest of moments, father and daughter . . . time that could never be recaptured. All too soon, the day came and he would not remember it. But she will always carry it in her heart. I am so thankful that she shared that memory with me. A picture in my mind and heart of the two of them together frozen in time before he died. What a gift.

I want to be more intentional about rubbing lotion on your feet. We may or may not talk. We can just be. And just like this morning . . . you will probably lean forward and look down my shirt, which is just fine with me. But here's the thing, I plan on you being around long enough so that one day you don't remember me doing this.

But I will remember it and smile.

The Hose

Last night when you were sitting on the back deck while I was watering the flowers, I was very tempted to turn the hose on you. For no reason, other than I could. You just seemed to be a good target. But your phone rang and distracted me, so I lost my chance.

The big pot of impatiens got me to thinking of what you are experiencing now. If they are watered, they bloom beautifully. But if I miss even a couple of days watering them, I can look out the kitchen window and see that they are all wilted and pitiful-looking. But once I turn the hose on and soak them good, they just perk right up and look beautiful once again.

The same theory can be applied to you and your dialysis. If you are getting your blood cleaned three days a week, you should feel good. But I know there will be periods of drought just like we have in the summer. And you will probably have times when you just won't feel so good after your treatment. That is to be expected. That is how life is at times. We can deal with that.

I remember hearing you and Big Daddy talk during those years when we needed the rain to fall on our farm. We could have used the irrigation system. Sometimes we had to because of the drought conditions. But I quickly learned from the two of you that the rain provided from above was much better for our crop than what came from the city or pumped out of the creek. I guess sometimes in life, as in farming, we just need the heavenly rain to fall on us.

Joker Poker

We have talked a lot lately about our plans and dreams—how things we thought we would be doing at this stage of life, we are not able to do. Things we planned have not happened, while other unplanned things have taken over our lives.

I guess it is sort of like the card game we play, Joker Poker. You lay out twelve cards face down. Turn over two cards. Then each of the players takes a turn pulling a card from the middle pile. The object is to line your cards up in two rows, matching cards side by side before any of the other opponents can. You can plan a strategy but then you get fed a card by the person next to you and your game is all out of whack . . . the best laid plans.

What a comfort it is to know that our Father has a master plan for our lives that is much grander than we could ever dream. We may not be able to wrap our minds around the purposes of all we are called to live through to experience the result of those plans, but I must believe that it will be worth it all.

> I know that you can do all things, and no plan of yours can be thwarted. (Job 42:2)

> But the plans of the LORD stand firm forever, the purposes of his heart through all generations. (Psalm 33:11)

Let's keep dreaming and planning.

God Is for Us

Earlier today I was driving in the car thinking about our little family—the six of us. There are issues we are each facing. Sometimes it seems that it is all just too much. We pray and pray, and it appears things are going to come together and then for whatever reason the door closes. Slams shut! I mean come on, God . . . what are we doing wrong here? Have we not prayed enough? Sacrificed enough? Waited long enough? When will it be our turn? Are you punishing us for some unconfessed sin? Oh, I know that's not how God operates. It's just in the moment, it is so hard not to feel it. When your children are bruised and battered, it's so difficult to sit and watch. When the love of your life is dealing with something you can't fix . . . and your personality is to fix things.

I do know that for whatever reason God closes the door to one thing, so that He can receive glory in other things. It is for our greater good that He works these things. I do know that in my head. It is just tonight, the heart of this wife and momma is hurting. I heard myself ask this question earlier today, "God, why are you against us?". And I was reminded of this verse from the NIV study Bible: *Romans 8:31, "What then shall we say in response to this? If God is for us, who can be against us?"*

I do believe His word. I do see evidences of His promises being fulfilled. But I admit . . . I am a drive thru, give-it-all-to-me-now, instant-gratification-sort-of girl. I need to be reminded every day of His faithful love for me.

And the good news is, regardless of what I feel or my unbelief, *God is for us!*

Stiff-Necked

Each Friday, an e-mail is sent to our entire church giving us the scripture passage for Sunday's Sermon. We are encouraged to read over it so that we can be prepared for the worship service.

We are currently in Exodus 33 and finishing up at verses 18 to 23 and then into chapter 34, verse 6 to 8. As I was reading the scriptures this morning, I continued reading past verse 8 in chapter 34 of Exodus, and it goes like this in the NIV Study Bible:

> Oh LORD, if I have found favor in your eyes," he said, "then let the LORD go with us. Although this is a stiff-necked people, forgive our wickedness and our sin, and take us as your inheritance." Then the LORD said; "I am making a covenant with you, before all your people I will do wonders never done in any nation in all the world. The people you live among will see how awesome is the work that I, the LORD, will do for you.

I have no idea what God intends to do in our situation—if His plan is to provide you with a new kidney for transplant, allow you to continue dialysis for thirty-five more years, or if it His plan is to glorify Himself through a total healing of your body in this life or in His presence. But I do know that we will see how awesome He is because of what He is doing right now. Not because of us . . . but because of Him. We are the stiff-necked, unbelieving people . . . *He is the faithful and true God.*

So again . . . I start all over today . . . praising *Him.* Renewing my mind and trusting. Believing that His word is true.

Doors and Windows

Even as doors are continuing to close for us and our children, there is fresh air that has unexpectedly begun to seep in at the bottom of some of our windows. When sometimes it has been hard to see the forest for the trees, with all our different and complicated situations—your health struggles, my tendency to borrow tomorrow's trouble today, financial and employment worries for us as well as our children, and the normal day-to-day challenges of being empty nester's—God is continuing to prove Himself to be a faithful God. He leads us to lush green pastures where we find rest. He provides us with quiet pools to drink from. He allows us to catch our breath before sending us on our way with the truth of His Word.

As we come to another door that has been closed, it is amazing how so often we are finding that He is also providing some form of encouragement to remind not just us . . . but also our children . . . that He is a faithful God. He will not fail us. We are also learning that *regardless of our circumstance in life, God is Good.* So we will praise Him for where He has us, even when it is difficult to do so. Even when "where we are" makes no sense to us.

Some doors that are being slammed in our faces are indeed an obvious blessing. God may be protecting us as well as our children by allowing many delays or just by flat out saying *no.* Other times God is providing protection to us in the fires of life. Sometimes we have found ourselves devastated and in a state of shock while there have been those times we could clearly see how God's hand was on a situation. It seems God often reveals to us much later an opportunity that had been hidden from our view. As if the answer had been there all along . . . if only we'd had our eyes open, or had been listening for His voice rather than suggesting a better or different outcome.

So tonight I must believe that God is doing a mighty work in the life of our entire family, that the closed doors and open windows He is placing in our lives are just one more opportunity for us to Praise Him from whom all blessings flow.

Closed doors and opened windows . . . both blessings.

Something New

Look I am about to do something new;
even now it is coming. Do you not see
it? Indeed, I will make a way in the wilderness, rivers in the desert.
                                        —Isaiah 43:19

There are so many days I feel as if I am wandering in the desert. Alone.

I am so ready for Him to do something new. To make a new way. To bring healing and restoration. I need fresh water to quench my thirsty heart, mind, body, and soul.

Options

We have many options on the table concerning our future.

It is overwhelming to consider them all at one time. To think that we are *even considering* these things now in our lives is overwhelming.

We are so very young. At least in *my* mind, but in truth we are. And that is the hard part. *We should not be here.*

Yet . . . here we are.

I look over at you, and I see someone who gives every outward appearance of being a healthy fifty-year-old man. But blood work and lab results do not lie.

You come home from dialysis, and you can hardly make it through the door. The process strips everything out of your blood. Leaving your body virtually starved. It takes you nearly twenty-four hours to recover from the process. Only to start all over again. How much longer can we hang on to the Tilt-O-Whirl before the carnival packs up and leaves town? It's with prayerful consideration that we weigh all our options. Taking each day as it comes and trusting God's plan.

Even though we don't understand it.

Let's Play Tennis

Each day we go out in the backyard and play tennis with Darby. We go through this same routine with her:

1. We hit the ball for her with the tennis racket.
2. She chases the ball.
3. She brings the ball back to where we are sitting comfortably in our seats.
4. She sloshes the ball around in her mouth then drops the ball on the racket.
5. We hit the ball for her, and the process starts all over again.
6. Wash, rinse, repeat.

But then there are times when she is in a mood . . . and she, for whatever reason, refuses to drop the ball on the tennis racket that is placed in front of her. It doesn't matter what we do or say. Wherever we hold the racket, she will drop the ball just to the right of the racket. Every. Single. Time.

It always makes us mad. Because, of course, that is not how we are supposed to play the game. She is supposed to obey us, bend to our will. Not her own.

A few minutes ago, the light bulb came on yet again, this whole scene played out. And I realized that this was in a way, a picture of my relationship with God. He is holding out His best for me. All I must do is place my faith . . . my trust . . . in Him.

But many times, I get so very close and then try to get Him to conform to my will. As if I can change His plan or bargain with God.

And just like I refuse to move that tennis racket and make that silly dog pick up the ball and place it where I want it, God is waiting on my obedience.

Waiting on me to follow Him. Waiting, patiently on me to stop selling out. Quit stopping short of His best. Settling for less than what He has planned for my life.

In this testing of our faith, I wonder what it is that He is having us learn. Is it just that we can trust Him? I wish that we would hurry up and learn that. Is it that we need to follow His plan, not our own. I wish we would figure that one out. Is it that His ways are perfect . . . ours lead to frustration, fear, and faithlessness.

Fall is in the air. I can see it and smell it. I am ready for this new season of the year . . . hoping that this changing of seasons brings about something new for us as well. A *good* new. A season of trusting God and seeking to joyfully enjoy and obey Him.

Trust . . . Again

Again, with the issue of trust. Is He trying to tell me something?

There is a devotional book on the shelf by my desk, *Grace for the Moment*[1] by Max Lucado. The entry for today is:

> "Don't let your hearts be troubled. Trust in God, and trust in me" (John 14:1).
>
> Our little minds are ill-equipped to handle the thoughts of eternity. When it comes to a world with no boundaries of space and time, we don't have the hooks for those hats. Consequently. Our Lord takes the posture of a parent . . . Trust me.

I think I have a better perspective on things this afternoon. Not that I am any nearer to being "okayer" if that is a word. Just that I am closer to getting a grip on things. For today anyway.

Changes are on the horizon. I am trusting that they are the right and good changes.

---

[1] Max Lucado, *Grace for the Moment*, Thomas Nelson, 1st Edition (March 2000).

Cheap Shirts

Yesterday was interesting. You came home with a huge blood stain on your shirt. Not just a spot. It covered your entire chest area on your left side. From your neck to your stomach . . . like a gunshot wound. Usually, you wear a button up shirt to dialysis. For some reason, you wore a golf shirt that is sort of banded near your elbows. So because you must keep your arm bandaged for twelve hours after each treatment, we could not take a chance of doing anything that would release the pressure on the bandage where the needle entered the fistula. We decided to cut the shirt off rather than keep it on for the next twelve hours just to save the shirt.

After a most unpleasant Friday blood cleaning, I was not holding out hope for today to be such a great day, which shows how weak my faith is because we can't ever live our lives based on the twenty-four hours we have just experienced. We must live in the present moment.

Sometimes things go wrong when you are at dialysis. Yesterday was one of those days. As you said while I was cutting the blood-stained shirt off you "I have had this cheap shirt for five years. I think I paid $15 for it at Wal-Mart. It does not matter anyway."

I appreciate your attitude. I know that this is hard for you. And I realize it is not getting any easier. But it is a new day. You could rest last night. We are going to make it through this. Regardless of how many shirts I must cut off you. After all, they are just cheap shirts.

Surgery

Fistula gram. Fistula Revision. New fistula. Ashland Catheter. Fistula Stent.

I guess the apprehension at what this week would possibly bring has been quickly addressed in one fail swoop. The whole bag of tricks so to speak.

Although I know it shouldn't, we've done this before, but our meeting with the surgeon today has left me just a tad overwhelmed. I know we agreed to do this, that it must be done. But suddenly, it is just so much to process at one time.

I guess if there was just a specific plan. You know, "we are going to do *this* and then be done. Forty-five-minute procedure and out." But the list of things that are possibly going to take place once you are asleep . . . it's just that once again we are back to the *not knowing*.

Wednesday will be a long day for you. Work. Dialysis. Surgery. I'll be here when you wake up.

The Riders on the Bus

It was June 1978.

We were on the trip to New York City with our youth choir.

We sat next to each other the entire time.

When we drew names for secret prayer partners you got my name.

I whined and complained the whole time when everyone else was getting little surprises and anonymous words of encouragement from their prayer partner and I got nothing.

On the last day, you gave me a sweet gift and revealed that you had my name.

When we got home, you asked me out for a date.

You picked me up in your metallic blue Camaro.

We went to Pizza Inn and to the movie . . . *The Jungle Book*.

From that night on, neither of us ever dated anyone else.

I am not sure why I thought back to that time just now.

Except to say . . . after all these years, I am still glad I sat next to you on the bus.

Difficult Days

I've been difficult to deal with today. Well, okay yes, for the last couple of days.

If we were both honest you have been too. But you have a much better excuse. Your arm has been ripped open and stitched back together. You are in pain.

But I am too.

I close my eyes and I keep seeing images of the older couple from Monday as I was waiting in the car while you finished up dialysis. They looked to be in their older seventies, and he had on an Auburn cap. I am sure he is the man you have spoken of before. He was in a wheelchair.

I watched as his wife slowly wheeled him to their truck and helped him into the passenger side. Then she wheeled the chair to the tailgate and lifted it into the back of the truck. Made her way to the driver side and then back around to his side to fasten his seatbelt.

It was a very sobering sight. My heart was in my throat. I was seeing our future.

Then you came out and we went to see the vascular surgeon, and he pronounced that you needed another surgery.

As I have said, I was prepared for this. He told us to expect additional surgery. So it was not a surprise. It's just that the last surgery took so long. It scared me. I tried to keep my "game face" on, but inside I was thinking the worst.

I am finding that it is exhausting trying to be Pollyanna all the time. I am just worn out. And difficult.

I know there are better days ahead. I know I should not look at our circumstances but rather keep my eyes and my focus on the Lord.

I know all the right things to say. All the right things to do. I know He will meet our every need. I don't doubt that. It is just that sometimes our circumstances are so overwhelming that it's just so easy to forget all that I do know. All the blessings of this moment that we do have.

I fear what the future could possibly bring.

You Light Up My Life

When I was sixteen, my favorite song was "You Light Up My Life." I would stand in my bedroom using a hairbrush as my microphone and pretend I was Debby Boone singing to my boyfriend of the moment. Because . . . at that moment he was lighting up my life. Until I extinguished the flame and moved on to some other guy who I then sang that song to, with my hairbrush microphone. All sixteen-year-old girls did this. I'm just confident, or foolish, enough to admit it.

I used your car today to run some errands, and I just happened to look in the backseat as I was unlocking the door. I guess you know there is an animal skull laying on the back seat. I'm sure it's the same one you said you found when you were mowing the property last week. Really . . . what good reason would you possibly have for driving around with it in your car?

Yes. You light up my life. But I may just have to beat you with my hairbrush microphone . . . you are a very weird man.

A Stitch in Time

Your arm looks mighty nasty. That raised red scar runs from your armpit all the way down past your elbow. It seems that for all his years in school and all his many surgeries, your surgeon could have at least stitched you up in a straight line.

I was thinking this afternoon how far we have come on this journey. Back in May, we were blissfully ignorant when the fistula was placed in your arm and you had just a small scar and only a few stitches. We thought you were at least two years away from using the fistula. Two years from additional surgery. Two years from dialysis.

Look at all we have been through. You have had that arm cut open four times since May. As of today, you have had forty-two dialysis treatments. I look back on this time, and I am amazed that we have done this. That we have lived this. That we still have so much more to live through.

There have been so many days. Good days and bad. Ups and downs and days in between that are just mundane days. But God continues to be faithful—not just when things are good and not only when we are faithful to Him. Even when we are not. When I look you in the eyes and ask "can we go back to before?", when it is not a good day at our house, when things are bad at our house, God is still faithful. He is meeting our needs.

His love is unfailing. His timing is perfect.

I will never grasp the depth of either.

This is a journey. I am glad we are on it together.

Girls Trip and Deer Skulls

Back in May when I was invited to go on an October girls trip, it seemed so easy to commit to. A lot has happened in five months.

I am so very excited about leaving tomorrow. But to be honest, I'm also a little bit nauseous. Excited because I cannot wait to be with my friends away from the hustle and bustle of life. Excited because I need the female companionship that a nine-day slumber party will bring. Excited about quaint little villages and window shopping, sitting in front of the fire doing nothing. Taking the ferry into Boston, going to Kennebunkport, Salem at Halloween, the fall foliage, historical tours, playing cards, reading—a much-needed girls trip.

But I am also somewhat anxious at the thought of being gone from home for this long. Leaving *you* for this long. This is just something that we do not do. Neither of us have ever traveled for our jobs. So we rarely have the occasion to be gone from each other or from home for long periods of time. And given our current situation, I am rather apprehensive to leave. It's the *what ifs* that concern me. But I realize those can take place any time, and I still would have no control over them. It is a trust issue between me and the Lord. Clearly, I get that.

But here's another thing . . . I think you need me to be gone. And I think I need me to be gone. Not in a bad way. Just in a *we-both-need-a break-from-me* sort of way. Because I think I am about to smother both of us. *And I know you need to breathe.* Does that make any sense at all? It sounded so logical until I typed it out.

I think you need a few days where I don't ask so many questions. Where you can just be. Days where I don't make my faces at you. And you don't just blankly stare back at me. And force me to get snarky.

Here's a thought. How about while I'm gone you get that eight-point deer skull out of the back seat of your car. Hang it on the wall in the den like you said you were planning to do. Enjoy looking at it for the next nine days. Then when I get back, we move it to the garage.

Yes. I do believe that works for me.

Here in the Real World

The problem with public journaling is that invariably there will be days when, like today, you feel like faking it. When you wish that you had not made that grand proclamation to be transparent and real.

Because in the day to day *life* of marriage and living, there are times when things are not so great. When the posting of that day's events may not shed the brightest of lights on you and your partner. So, faking it or flat out lying is the best option.

Today you were successful in pushing my buttons. Admittedly, I was *a little* sensitive. I probably made an easy target. So my first instinct tonight is to just make up something that sounds happy. Or find a verse from my yet-to-be-done Bible study and make it fit. But that is not what this is about.

Real life. The good. The bad. The ugly that we are. The joys and the struggles. Triumphs that we work our way through. And our heavenly Father that we cling to, to guide us on this journey that we call our life. And every aspect of it.

I am so thankful for a fresh start each morning. Hopefully tomorrow will be a better day.

If Only

I must admit, during this whole process we have been going through I have been wondering how we could have done things differently. Is there something we could have done to achieve a different outcome? I know in my head that you have a disease that without God's intervention is incurable. But I still find myself so many occasions thinking that there must have been something that we could have done.

"If only we had done this or that."

"If only this drug had been introduced earlier."

Yesterday I started reading a new book. Well, new to me anyway. *Trusting God Even When Life Hurts*[2] by Jerry Bridges. In his book, he makes a point that got me to thinking.

> *Our lives are cluttered with a lot of "if onlys." . . . "If only I had done this" or "if only that had not happened." But again, God has no if onlys. God never makes a mistake; God has no regrets. As for God, his way is perfect (Psalm 18:30). We can trust God. He is trustworthy.*

In the chapter I just finished, he reminds us that in times of adversity our priority is to honor and glorify God by trusting Him. Even though our natural tendency is to make our priority the gaining

---

[2] Jerry Bridges, *Trusting God When Life Hurts,* NavPress, First Edition (March 2009).

of relief from our feelings of heartache or disappointment or frustration. God has given us grace sufficient for our trials and peace for our anxieties.

If only I could learn to glorify Him by trusting Him.

Bruised

I find it more than a little ironic that just yesterday at the transplant seminar we attended, we were told more than once that things can go wrong in dialysis. Even when using the preferred AV fistula, which you have.

The speaker talked about the different kinds of access and the problems with each. Several times he made the point that our bodies were not made for needles to be inserted in the veins multiple times each week. That at some point the vein will be missed . . . resulting in bruising.

Whenever I have had any medical procedures or the need for an IV, it is not uncommon for me to notice bruising the next day. You can almost look cross-eyed at my momma, and she will bruise up even quicker than I do. Some people are just built that way. Today they missed your vein, and you came home with a small water balloon protruding from the upper portion of your forearm. It's bruised. It looks awful and painful. Usually you don't seem to think much of things like this. But I can tell it is bothering you. Mainly because you said so.

I am so tired of brushing everything off to "this is just part of the process." But I guess it just is. One more thing we must adjust to. Sometimes they miss. And you bruise. *Bad.*

As I type the word *bruise* over and over, the passage in Isaiah 53[3] is playing in my mind . . .

---

[3] Isaiah 53 King James Version

> *But he was wounded for our transgressions, he was bruised for our iniquities: the chastisement of our peace was upon him; and with his stripes we are healed.*

He took my place, *that* is the heart of the gospel. *That* is what the "good news" is about. He bears my transgressions, so that their weight will not overwhelm me. He was beaten for my iniquities. And He crushed them when He rose from the grave. When I should be chastised and whipped for my rebellion; He took that on Himself so that I could have freedom and healing.

Praying that tonight we will both find rest in His sacrificial love.

Chaos

Our life feels chaotic at times. There are days when I wonder how we will ever make it through to the next day. I think we would feel this way without kidney disease, if you want to know the truth. We as humans tend to get caught up in the business of living our lives rather than *living as God intended us to.*

If only we could learn to totally surrender to Him. Not just our hearts. But our everyday lives. So that the chaos could become peace. So we could clean house, spiritually speaking. Breathe in and let everything out. Learn to follow Him so that we are not climbing aimlessly over hills. Begin experiencing something larger than life. Something heavenly.

As we wait to see what the Lord has for us, I must tell you I am somewhat excited but it's mixed in with a touch of apprehension. I am so ready for Him to do something new with us. To honor His promises. Fulfill His word . . . not that I'm saying He is on a time schedule with me. It's just been many years that we started this specific personal, business, and financial journey. I am weary of praying every day, "Lord make it so today. Let this be the day if this is your will. Honor your words today."

Thank you for your consistent and level-headed wisdom. In all the chaos that I sometimes feel, you are a calming influence on me.

Thanksgiving 2009

Documenting the days on this journey, I have come to realize that we are blessed. Very blessed. Why God would choose to throw open the windows of heaven and rain down His showers of blessing on our lives is a mystery to me. I am the first to admit that on so many days I take for granted the gifts in our lives. I only look at what I want. What we do not have. Where we are not. All too often I fail to look with a heart of thankfulness for what we have been given.

It is so easy to become so consumed in the circumstances of our own existence that we fail to see the hurting of those around us. I do it all the time. I am doing it right now. I believe it is sometimes called tunnel vision. We can dress it up with all kinds of cute little names, but the reality is we are not thankful for what we have. Otherwise we would look beyond ourselves. Our own needs. Our own wants and desires. Into the lives of others who are hurting and needing. We would begin to focus our time and energies on someone other than ourselves.

I am of the belief that this is what a thankful heart does. This is what a thankful life looks like. It is my desire that I would be described this way. But I make no grand promises that from today on I will live a life that reflects one of self-sacrifice. I seriously doubt I will ever be called upon to give my life for someone else while going about my day to day living. But I will commit to living with a more *thankful spirit* for how the Lord has chosen to bless me. Realizing that everything I have is a gift from Him. That my very existence is meant to bring Him alone glory.

Because when it is all said and done, this journey we are on is not about you or me. It is about Him. It is about His faithfulness. It has little to do with kidney disease but is truly about the God who formed man out of dust from the ground and breathed into his nostrils the breath of life.

Our story is about the One who sacrificed His own Son to set each of us free from our sin and misery. And that is something to be thankful for as we enter this season . . . and every day.

A Ring and a Win

It was thirty years ago today. Do you remember?

You were laid off from work at the farm for the winter. So you did what any budget-minded, disciplined young man planning for his future would do. You cashed your entire unemployment check (remember . . . they used to pay those out in one lump sum back then) and you bought an engagement ring.

On December 1, 1979, you proposed to me. For the second time. The first time, I squealed yes, but my daddy said no. I am not sure if it was because you did not have a ring or if it was because I had only been out of high school three months.

But on this day thirty years ago, you asked again.

He did say yes.

And so, did I.

Again.

Come to think of it . . . maybe "the yes" was because Daddy came home from the Iron Bowl so happy that Alabama had beaten Auburn 25–18, and he would have agreed to anything! Maybe he was giving me away to the first boy who came by, and you got stuck with me. Have you ever looked at it like that? Remember . . . he also promised you that you would get the pool table when he said that you could have me. Turns out you only got to keep the pool table for about a year. But you have been stuck with me for a lot longer than that!

Oh, well. Ring or win. Daddy finally said yes.

And after thirty years, I'm still glad you asked.

Where is God?

"Many hundreds of years ago, the prophet Habakkuk struggled with the question of "where is God?" in all the evil that he saw around him. He finally concluded that, though he did not understand what God was doing, he would trust Him. His affirmation of trust, couched in the language of a world falling apart around him, would be a fitting example for us to follow as we struggle with God's sovereignty" (Jerry Bridges).[4]

> *Though the fig tree does not bud*
> *and there are no grapes on the vines,*
> *Though the olive crop fails*
> *and the fields produce no food,*
> *Though there are no sheep in the pen*
> *and no cattle in the stalls,*
> *Yet I will rejoice in the* LORD,
> *I will be joyful in God my Savior.*
> *(Habakkuk 3:17–18)*

Just as I am about to give up . . . *because we have established already that I only see today, not the big picture* . . . we get a phone call from our Nashville kids. Things are going so well for them. The excitement in their voices is such an encouragement to my heart. To hear their words and know that during the normal struggles of start-

---

4   Jerry Bridges, *Trusting God in a World of Hurt,* NavPress (January 2006).

ing their careers they are so encouraged by the doors that are being opened to them is such a blessing right now.

Doors that only He could open. He is proving Himself faithful. Generation to generation. So even though we may be tempted to ask "where is God?" because our circumstances so blind us to His presence, the answer is simple. He is right where He has always been. He has never left our side.

Day 150

We've now been in this new unpredictable, maddening, soul crushing, mind numbing phase of life for 150 days. I feel as if I should write something profound here.

But we've had a rather crummy day. You and I again had some "communication issues." And being the mature human being I am, you made me mad when we were on the phone, so I hung up on you.

Yes . . . I am forty-eight and still in the sixth grade.

One day we will get it right.

I am looking forward to a better day tomorrow and hoping that we soon get out of this funk that seems to have overtaken us.

New Year's Eve

It is that time of the year when everywhere you look you see ads about New Year's resolutions. And it is that time of the year when I traditionally resolve not to make any resolutions. Because let's be real . . . my track record is historic for epic failure.

Honestly, our current situation scares me. Our future . . . those older people I see going into the dialysis center, they don't encourage me. I look at them, and that's the future I see for you. For me as your caregiver. When I flashback to that silly nineteen-year-old girl standing in that size 7 white wedding dress looking at the love of her life and vowing for better or worse, richer or poorer, in sickness or health . . . it never occurred to me that we would be doing *this,* even though I didn't have a clue what *this* was. I thought you just had a kidney infection.

Failing at *this* is my biggest fear right now . . . failing you. Not being or doing enough to make it just one more day. Having those dialysis friends show up one day and hear that *you* won't be back. Having the family and friends who faithfully turn on their computers and read about our life no longer have anything to read about. No more random texts from you that say "i miss u" during a busy day. Missing the sound of your laughter with our kids in the den when they are all home. No longer watching you and Darby in the backyard.

Oh, I do know that our sovereign Lord has determined our days and has a perfect plan for our lives. I know that I could exhaust myself and wear you out in the process of trying to do enough to keep you alive. When really the heart of my issue is *trust*. Am I trusting this sovereign One who has from the beginning of time determined your days? I know all the right things to say. *But do I trust Him?* I have given Him my heart. *But do I trust Him with my life . . . with my family?*

So this is where we get back to my resolution for 2010. In this coming year, I want to come to know my Savior. Because how can you truly trust someone who you have not fully developed a genuine relationship with? I grew up in the church. I have been afforded every advantage there is from a Christian standpoint. Yet I find myself so often taking my Christian heritage for granted. My most earnest hope is that in the process of developing a more genuine relationship with my Lord in this new year, I will be able to release these fears I am clinging to concerning you. Concerning our future. Concerning us. Concerning me.

Our future life is too precious. The possibilities of joyful service are too great for us to not be trusting God . . . knowing Him as He desires that we know Him. After all, He is our Father and we are His children.

My Dwelling Place

I have not talked much lately about how you are feeling right now. You have done well at dialysis. You've not had a reason to cut off any clothing when you come home . . . so that is good. I think you have started to settle into a rhythm with everything. I will admit that I can't help looking over our shoulder from time to time for fear that something or someone will catch us.

Your sleep schedule is rather odd. You seem to wake after only an hour or two each night then go back to bed for several hours then wake for your day. I still cannot believe it is restful or helpful to you. But this is our life right now.

Early this morning I began to think about something I read a few days ago, concerning how we view God. So often I have thought of God as this supreme being and not a place to dwell. This majestic miracle worker that I turn to when I am desperate and need a quick fix, but not a place to live. He is the Creator, but not a home where I would reside.

But God the Father desires to be so much more. He wants to be the One in whom *"we live and move and have our being" (Acts 17:28).*[5]

I guess it is like the house in the woods that you and I want to build. We dream about it. We talk about it. We plan for it. But until we dig the foundation, build the house, and take up residence there . . . what good is it? How many times can I look at house plans on the computer . . . I still don't live there. The flowers are not grow-

---

[5] Acts 17:28 English Standard Version.

ing in the yard. We are not sitting on the back porch watching the sunset or feeling the cool fall breeze.

God wants to be our dwelling place.

He wants to be *our home*.

I am ready for Him to be my home.

Restoration

I have been thinking about healing. Praying for a complete healing for you. Not just for you to get be to better. But restored. Here, with me.

In his book, *Grace for the Moment,*[6] Max Lucado says, *"God loves to decorate. God has to decorate. Let Him live long enough in a heart, and that heart will begin to change. Portraits of hurt will be replaced by landscapes of grace. Walls of anger will be demolished and shaky foundations restored. God can no more leave a life unchanged than a mother can leave her child's ear untouched."*

> This might explain some of the discomfort in your life. Remodeling of the heart is not always pleasant. We don't object when the Carpenter adds a few shelves, but He's been known to demolish the entire west wing. He has such high aspirations for you. God envisions a complete restoration. He won't stop until He is finished. He wants you to be just like Jesus.

As much as I keep trying to make this about a kidney, I continue to believe this is really about restoration of our hearts.

---

[6]   Max Lucado, *Grace for the Moment*, Thomas Nelson 1st Edition (March 2000).

Tennessee River Fog

As I drove across the Tennessee River Bridge this afternoon, I noticed what I thought was fog, which seemed odd for two in the afternoon. I kept taking my sunglasses off to look at the river as I drove across just to see if what I saw was what I saw. And there it was.

There were boats on the water. And fishermen there in the fog. Over some parts of the water was sunshine. But then over a large portion there was a great amount of fog.

It seemed symbolic of my life for some of these last six months. There have been times when everything seemed all sunshine and roses. When, for lack of a better way to say it . . . I have been basking in the glow of God's faithfulness and my surety of His being there for us. Confident in His plan for our lives.

Other days I have been lost in the fog. A deep, thick fog. There have been days that I can only explain as gray days for me. I have always known that the fog would lift or would not last because just like on the river today where I could see rays of sunshine off in the distance. Even on the darkest days I know He is there even when I cannot see Him or feel Him. Past experiences with Him give me great confidence that He will not fail us. He will not forsake us. Possibly our rescue will not be according to our timetable, but *our rescue will come from the Lord.*

This new normal we are transitioning to . . . it is still taking some getting used to. Even six months in I still at times feel shell shocked when I wake up in the middle of the night and realize what we are dealing with. The gravity of it is overwhelming when I think long term.

The things that are constantly being introduced into your daily life, they effect both of us. Maybe not me so much in a physical way as they do you, but more so in an emotional way. You seem to be adjusting fine. You seem to always be doing great. I on the other hand feel as if I am living life on a roller coaster emotionally. And the ride takes random trips through the fog on the river and comes out in the sunshine on the other side. Only to slip back into the fog when I am not looking. Am I being a touch dramatic? Probably. However, at this moment there is no other way to describe it.

Thank you for constantly paddling through the fog, throwing me a rope and pulling my boat back into the sunshine.

Sleepless in Alabama . . . Still

Second verse. Same as the first.

This new year has brought a new concern. You don't sleep. You have taken over-the-counter and under-the-counter sleep meds. Yet you are still unable to sleep. You say over the last forty-eight hours, you have probably had about four hours of restful sleep.

You've come to the den and entertained me with your impression of Christina Aguilera, Rascal Flatts, and several other singers.

You've gone into the kitchen and burned bacon and then appeared to be hurt when I turned my nose up at it. You change the channels from what I am watching on TV. You have stumbled back to the bedroom and now here you come again . . .

Even the dog knows something is wrong.

For His Glory

As you went to bed, I prayed a quick prayer that you would be able to sleep again tonight. Last night you could get some rest for an extended period. In fact, I had decided not to wake you up for church this morning because you were sleeping so soundly. But at the last minute, you woke up and although we were late, we did make it there.

You have had a rough week. A weird week. I don't know if it is one of your meds messing up your sleep or maybe they just need to be tweaked a bit. Hopefully whatever it is can be adjusted or maybe it's worked itself out. This is again part of the fine tuning we are having to do. I am sorry you have had such a tough time and that I could not do anything but be here.

I was reading in my *Trusting God Even When Life Hurts*[7] book this evening. I had put it aside at the end of the year and only in the last couple of days picked it back up. Jerry Bridges is talking about illness and physical affliction in the pages I am reading. Seems appropriate. He says the following:

> *Illness and physical affliction is an area in which we struggle to trust God. When God called Moses to lead the Israelites out of Egypt, Moses protested his inadequacy, including the fact that he was slow of speech. God's reply to Moses is very instruc-*

---

[7] Jerry Bridges, *Trusting God Even When Life Hurts,* NavPress First Edition (March 2008)

> *tive to us in this area of physical affliction, for God said "Who gave man his mouth? Who makes him deaf or mute? Who gives him sight or makes him blind? Is it not I, the LORD?" (Exodus 4:11). Here God specifically ascribes to His own work the physical afflictions of deafness, muteness, and blindness.*

Afflictions don't "just happen." They are all within the sovereign will of God. God never wastes pain. He always uses it to accomplish His purpose. And His purpose is for His glory and our good. Therefore, we can trust Him when our hearts are aching or our bodies are racked with pain."

I know that I have referred to his statement that "*God never wastes pain*" several times before. He repeats the phrase several times throughout the book. Maybe this is something important for us to remember.

This is for His glory. And your good. He used Moses. He will use you as well.

Remember

When you can't sleep and the leg cramps are awful like they were last night, remember . . .

We know He is there.

This is for His glory and our good.

Everything works in accordance to His sovereign will.

We have a hope in Him.

He is our strength and refuge.

He is for us and not against us.

He is our comforter.

He never leaves us . . .

This Just Stinks

This incessant sleeplessness is getting old. Hopefully it will be resolved soon, as I am beginning to feel guilty when I fall asleep and do not wake until the appointed time the next morning

Sometimes it just stinks to have this disease. I guess there is no good time to have end stage renal failure. It is just that the *other little things* that go along with the big stuff you deal with, are so annoying. And sometimes it is those *other little things* that are so blasted demanding of your time and energy.

I know you are frustrated. I know you are tired. I know you want this to be over and yet we both know that "this"—without miraculous intervention from God—will never be "over."

And sometimes, most times . . . that just stinks. I wish I could make it better. I wish I could be more encouraging.

Beauty from Ashes

Once again, I find myself back in Jerry Bridges book, *Trusting God Even When Life Hurts.*[8] I cannot seem to finish it. Or completely put it down.

"God's infinite wisdom is then displayed in bringing good out of evil, beauty out of ashes. It is displayed in turning all the forces of evil that rage against His children into good for them."

But the good that He brings about is often different from the good we envision.

When I began documenting our journey, I could not fathom all we have been through in the almost seven months. In the grand scheme of a lifetime, this is a very short period. But in the living of the days, I look back on this time and wonder how we have come this far.

I can clearly see the handprint of God in so many instances. Times when His Word has been so clear. But then, on so many occasions He was silent. It is in His silence that I have been stretched to trust Him the most. To trust what I *know* rather than what I *feel.* Trusting that He will turn this time of our life into good despite our circumstances. And that in this, we will learn to praise Him.

May you and I truly see the good and the beauty as God intends for us to see it. Regardless of how it is brought to us.

---

[8] Jerry Bridges, *Trusting God Even When Life Hurts,* NavPress First Edition (March 2008)

About this Morning

This morning at 3:15, you patted me on the back and quietly whispered, "I am going to drive myself to the ER because I am having chest pains . . ."

That is not the beautiful Sunday I had imagined when I looked at the weather forecast on the ten o'clock news before coming to bed last night.

Obviously, the Lord had other plans for our day. Our life. *A heart attack*. I guess we just had nothing better going on right now. So tonight you are in the ICU awaiting further evaluation tomorrow. Most likely a procedure to correct the damage done.

Isn't it a comfort to know that our days were measured and planned long before we ever drew our first breath? And when the difficult days come, He provides the strength we need to get through each of them every step of the way.

I have no clue what the days ahead may hold for us.

But I know who holds the days.

Life on Loan

"The Bible reveals to us that life is given freely to us by God (Acts 17:25, Job 1:21). Life is not something we possess by virtue of our merit. We do not "own" our life in relation to God. It is a "loan," as is implied in Luke 12:20 where the soul (life) is required "back" by the Lord. Life is God's and is on loan to us freely so that we might enjoy glorifying God with it. It is always and totally at his disposal never rightfully at our disposal (John Piper, A Godward Life).[9]

Life belongs to God.

Events such as what we are presently living through give us even greater pause to look at life in a more sobering manner. We are reminded that as His rightful possession, life is God's to take when He pleases. He does not need to consult anyone because His authority as the Creator and Sustainer of life puts it totally at His disposal. He is not doing any evil when He takes back the life He gave whenever He chooses.

Our lives are so much richer because you were *loaned* to us for a season of time. We are each devastated. Our hearts are broken. The

---

[9] John Piper, *A Godward Life: Savoring the Supremacy of God in All of Life,* Multnomah Publishers (September 1997).

reality of this situation comes and goes. Maybe it has not yet begun to sink in. But when our practical minds take over, we realize that you are at peace . . . and so for the briefest of moments we are finding peace in that.

December 27, 1958–February 22, 2010.

Let's Just Praise the Lord

In the Old Testament recordings of Job, in chapter 11 verses 7 to 9, Job asks, *"Can you fathom the mysteries of God? Can you probe the limits of the Almighty?' They are higher than the heavens above— what can you do? They are deeper than the depths below—what can you know? Their measure is longer than the earth and wider than the sea."*

I wish that I knew the mind of God or could at least tell you that I understand why the events of later today must take place. I am by nature a planner. I get that from my parents, so I guess I come by it honestly. I like to know each day of the week where I am going and I like to know what is expected of me. I keep a list so that I can know when I have performed each day or each week's tasks. But I must tell you last Friday at work, when I was calendaring my events for this week . . . standing at a grave with my husband's name on it was not on that list.

But what a wonderful gift it is to know that God is never caught off guard by the events that take place in my life. To be totally honest, I have struggled with that concept in these last few hours. At every turn, I have questioned His love for me. I have wondered why He didn't step in and change things so that my week, my life, could have gone on like I had it so neatly mapped out.

But then my mind keeps going back to Jeremiah 29:11 where His word tells me . . . *"For I know the plans I have for you says the Lord . . . to give you a hope."* And then over to Romans 8 where He assures me that He is *"working all things for my good."*

At one thirty this morning, I woke up to a moment of desperation, and I was thinking that this Gospel we believe in . . . it had better be true. We have no hope without it! At least that much I know is an essential truth. But if I'm honest, on so many days it is a truth I take for granted and don't treat with proper respect and urgency. But in these last few days, I find I am hanging on to that truth for my next breath.

I can listen to that voice of doubt whispering in my ear "where was your God four days ago?", "how could your loving God allow you to hurt this way?"; or I can cling to the truth that I know. I do have a hope in Him. He is working for my good, even when I cannot see it or feel it just yet. Even when it does not make sense to me. When my heart is so broken, I think I cannot possibly go on. When I consider the faces of those I love so dearly and I cannot heal their unspeakable pain. The only comfort I can offer them is . . . Jesus is real. God's word is true. And despite our earthly circumstances that seem to contradict, I know that He is a good and sovereign God who can be trusted.

Job was correct . . . I can't fathom the mysteries of God. I can't probe the limits of the Almighty. He is higher than the heavens. He is deeper than the depths of the grave. He is longer than the earth and wider than the sea. And yet, His love for me is also beyond measure.

I continue to remind myself, if I am trusting this God with my eternal salvation, how can I not trust Him just one day, one hour at a time? So I will trust Him and I will praise Him. Because this is my *only* choice.

In Jeremiah 29, the scriptures go on to tell us in verses 13 and 14, "*You will call upon me and come and pray to me, and I will listen to you. You will seek me and find me when you seek me with all your heart. I will be found by you,' declares the Lord.*"

Today, as we gather with family, friends, and coworkers to celebrate your life, your family chooses to praise the LORD for His love and faithfulness and His promise to meet us where we are.

Big Love

Thursday morning at ten thirty, we had a family service for you. There in the cemetery on land that was long ago donated by my great-grandfather . . . your body was laid to rest near those who have gone before you. Those dear ones who have loved me and poured their lives into mine. Spent hours in the blazing heat maintaining their crops to keep their family fed. Rising early in the morning before the light of the day to milk their cows and gather eggs. But always after spending time in the Word and in prayer with the Lord.

I find no coincidence in the fact that you have spent the last years of your life rising early in the morning before the light of the day, to support your family. You are not a reader. It's no secret, you are an auditory learner. You have loaded the Bible onto your laptop and your iPod. It was a common occurrence for me to find you with your iPod listening to the Word. Hiding it in your heart. Thank you for that gift!

Do you have a clue how your life has impacted your world? I think you probably don't. It has been so comforting to read the comments from your friends and coworkers. You loved big, and you were loved big in return. And now, your family is being loved big. Thank you for that gift!

Your body is there where you had said for so long you wanted it to be when this day came. We are comforted by the knowledge that as you breathed your last breath, you opened your eyes in the presence of our sovereign Savior. There is no more pain for you, it is finished. The battle is over, and victory has been won.

However, our pain is still fresh, deep, and big. But our God loves deep and big. And we have an assurance that although our hearts have been ripped open and the days ahead will be long, we are not alone as we begin to walk this new path that we have been called to. We will continue to trust Him as He leads us on this journey. Step by step.

I'll See Ya Later

Early Tuesday morning, just a handful of hours after your death, I was laying in our bed . . . which, even with April restlessly sleeping next to me, has suddenly become so very huge. I began to beat myself up for not staying in the room with you longer than I did.

It was 3:15, when we said goodbye. The visiting time for ICU started at 2:30, and the nurse whispered that I could stay as long as I wanted. She told me not to worry about the fifteen-minute rule, that no one would ask me to leave.

We had been talking, and you were being your normally goofy self. You didn't seem to be in any pain. We talked about our children. You said some very sweet things to me about us and our life together. You asked if anyone had gone home to let Darby out and throw the tennis ball for her. Always worried about your faithful companion. You asked if I had posted an update on Facebook. And I said your friends were praying and sending their prayers like crazy. That you were loved like no one I had ever seen.

Then I remember looking up at the clock and at 3:15, I said, "I guess I should go now." You didn't ask me to stay. You just pulled me close with your left arm, grabbed my backside, patted it, grinned, and laughed. Then pulled me closer into you and kissed me real big. Winked at me and smiled. I said, "Goodbye, baby," and you said, "I'll see ya later . . ."

As I left the room, the nurse you had quickly nicknamed Ginger, because of her long red hair, came in and took your hand. I looked back at both of you, and she was standing where I had just been, holding the hand I had just let go of. My last memory is hearing you laugh at something she said. That same nurse would later tell me, with tears streaming down her cheeks, that while you were laughing things began to go very wrong. Your doctors were immediately called in, but all their efforts to save you were unsuccessful. Your death certificate will say that your life here on earth ended at 4:08 p.m., Monday, February 22, 2010.

What a precious gift we were given in those forty-five minutes on Monday afternoon. We said goodbye on our terms, it was not rushed. There were no interruptions. We didn't know it was our last goodbye. It was natural . . . *and it was a good goodbye.*

But more beautiful than our goodbye is the knowledge that *this isn't goodbye. We haven't lost you at all. We know right where you are. We* just aren't there with you yet.

In this moment, that is what we are clinging to. That is where we find our comfort.

Laughter

Crisis times are odd times really. We find ourselves going from a moment of literally having to hold each other up to keep from falling on the ground, to all out-belly busting laughter within seconds. You, my sweet man, you have provided us with so many opportunities to laugh over these hours.

You lived a life full of laughter. Time and time again the comment to us has been how much your laugh will be missed. A person cannot genuinely laugh without a smile on their face, or so I have been told. And you had the most genuine robust laugh of anyone I have ever known.

Oh, let's be very clear . . . there were *many times* when your laugh irritated the stew out of me. When you laughed at things or times that were completely inappropriate. Or when you thought *yourself* to be funny, and you were not.

Yes, you were such a goofball. But you were mine. And I am grasping at anything to figure out how to get through the next hour without you.

Grieving with Hope

How do you survive the death of the love of your life . . . without Christ?

How can you even try to carry on after the rest of the world has returned to *their normal*, when your world is upside down . . . if you don't know the sovereign Savior?

In the stillness of the night, when the rest of your home is soundly sleeping and the left side of your king size bed is cold, empty and undisturbed who do you talk to . . . if you have no personal relationship with Jesus?

Yesterday, in a long conversation with your mom, we discussed whether either of us or your children, had experienced feelings of being mad at God. I was stunned that someone had asked her that question. The thought had never occurred to me. Even now after I have had time to process that thought, I can honestly say that although I look around at my current situation . . . *I rejoice for you!*

We prayed for your healing. And God answered our prayers. Although His plan did not include healing you according to *my plan or timing* . . . God has been faithful to His promises. He has blessed us beyond measure.

Stephen Curtis Chapman so perfectly described it in his song "With Hope."

This is not at all how we thought it was supposed to be.
We had so many plans for you, we had so many dreams.
But now you've gone away and left us with the memories of your smile.
And nothing we can say and nothing we can do,
can take away the pain of losing you.
And we can cry with hope.
We say goodbye with hope.
'Cause we know our good bye is not the end.
And we can grieve with hope, 'cause we believe with
hope, there's a place where we'll see your face again.
And I have never known anything so hard to understand.
And never have I questioned the wisdom of God's plan.
But through the cloud of tears I see the Father smile and say "well done."
And I imagine you where you wanted most to be.
Seeing all your dreams come true 'cause now
your home and now your free.
We have this hope as an anchor 'cause we believe
that everything God promised us is true.
We wait with hope and we ache with hope we hold on with hope.
We let go with hope.

Not Today

I keep thinking that one day I won't have to wake up and call my daddy and ask, *"Daddy . . . is it really true?"*

And he won't have to answer with tears streaming down his face and a quiver in his voice, *"Yes, babe . . . I'm afraid it is."*

Today was not that day. Why is this still so hard to believe? Why does this seem like fresh news every morning? Or whenever I get busy doing something mindless and then I suddenly remember?

That awful feeling in my gut reappears as if I am hearing those terrible words for the first time . . . all over again. I know others who have gone through this. They survived. I know I will as well. I'm just not sure about today.

Broken and bruised . . .

And missing you like crazy.

Tomorrow

Today's reading in *My Utmost for His Highest* (the updated version) says, "*Undiminished radiance, which is the result of abundant joy, is not built on anything passing but on the love of God that nothing can change. And the experiences of life, whether they are everyday events or terrifying ones, are powerless to "separate us from the love of God which is in Christ Jesus our Lord" (Romans 8:39).*

Tomorrow I go back to work. I need to be in my office, I have people who are waiting on me to take care of them. I need the distraction of a routine. A new routine, a different routine.

But . . . I don't want to go back yet. I am physically and mentally exhausted. I feel like I could sleep for another week. But if I waited another week . . . I would say I wasn't ready then. So I may as well start *my new* . . . tomorrow.

I need the distraction. *I need to not think.*

Tomorrow will be the first day I come home, and you won't be here waiting.

> *Answer me, O LORD, for Your loving kindness is good;*
> *According to the greatness of Your compassion, turn to me,*
> *And do not hide Your face from Your servant,*
> *For I am in distress; answer me quickly.*
> *Oh draw near to my soul and redeem it;*
> *Ransom me because of my enemies! (Psalm 69:16–18)*[10]

---

[10] Psalm 69:16–18 New American Standard

Tomorrow, give me your undiminished radiance and your abundant joy. Remind my heart of what my head knows . . . that nothing can change your love. Hear my cry for mercy. Be near to me and love me O LORD.

Hurting

It is one thing to deal with *my pain.*

It is all together a different kind of pain to watch those I love grieve so deeply.

So profoundly.

I hear it in April's voice all the way from Aspen, so far from home and alone. *She sounds homesick. And I am not there. She is hurting.*

I watch it in Ali's actions. She doesn't know what to do with me. *She is trying to protect me. She is hurting.*

I see it in Amy's e-mails. *She wants me in Nashville . . . with her. She is hurting.*

I read it in Andrew's text messages. *Just a few words . . . but I hear what is behind them. He's hurting as well.*

Our adult children miss their daddy. Oh, how I miss my children's daddy!

Your mom is being so brave, her faith is so strong. *But her heart misses her son. She is hurting.*

I see the pain in my own parent's eyes as they want desperately to say or do something for us. While dealing with their own grief . . . they have lost a son as well. *They are hurting.*

Your brother. Your sisters. Your family. Our friends. Our church. Everyone I meet . . . *hurting.*

Fifteen days. It hurts like fifteen months . . .

"May your unfailing love rest upon us, O LORD, even as we put our hope in you" (Psalm 33:22).

Incomprehensible

In the last three and a half weeks, I have had many conversations with many people who have said, *"I don't understand why it had to be Tom."* I understand their questioning. I have asked it myself. Many times, over.

I cannot fathom how any answer will ever be right or good enough to justify the pain. How any answer will ever make it okay. In fact, it seems incredibly wrong to even type that last sentence. Last night, I was back reading *Trusting God Even When Life Hurts*. Jerry Bridges says, *"We must learn to trust God when He doesn't tell us 'why,' when we don't understand what He is doing."*

God's ways are incomprehensible . . . sometimes we are almost insatiable in our quest for the why of the adversity that has come upon us. But that is a futile as well as an untrusting task. God's ways, being the ways of infinite wisdom, simply cannot be comprehended by our finite minds.

"'For my thoughts are not your thoughts, neither are your ways my ways,' declares the LORD. As the heavens are higher than the earth, so are my ways higher than your ways and my thoughts than your thoughts" (Isaiah 55:8–9)[11]

In his commentary on Isaiah, Edward J. Young said of this passage, *"The implication is that just as the heavens are so high above the earth that by human standards their height cannot be measured, so also are God's ways and thoughts so above those of man that they cannot be grasped by man in their fullness."*[12]

---

[11] Isaiah 55:8–9, English Standard Version
[12] Edward J Young, Isaiah, Eerdmans (December 1992)

In other words, the ways and thoughts of God are incomprehensible to man.

Charles H. Spurgeon said, *"Providence is wonderfully intricate. Ah! You want always to see through* Providence, *do you not? You never will, I assure you. You have not eyes good enough. You want to see what good that affliction was to you; you must believe it. You want to see how it can bring good to the soul; you may be enabled in a little time; but you cannot see it now, you must believe it. Honor God by trusting Him."*

Honor God by trusting Him. Trusting Him, even when life hurts. This hurts. It hurts more than I knew I had the capacity to hurt. The pain is incomprehensible. But I am learning that God's love for me is also incomprehensible.

Missing you so much that it hurts physically . . .

Widow

I do not like my new identity. I did not marry you to become your widow.

I am a wife. I am a mom. *This is what I have always wanted to be.*

The last Sunday of twelfth grade Sunday School, we were asked where we planned to be in ten years. My answer was that I would be married to you with three children. Ten years later, we had been married for nine years and we had four children. One of our babies was a bonus blessing from God, I will let them argue over which one.

In the last four weeks, I have been called *your widow* too many times! I still want to be your wife!

Beloved.

I have been chosen by Christ . . . He has claimed me as His beloved.

My identity in Him will never change.

Although my dreams came true when we married and I became the mother of your children, I much prefer my identity in Christ. I*t is secure.* It cannot be taken away from me by the cruelty and pain of death.

> *And behold, I am with you always, to the end of the age. (Matthew 28:20, ESV)*
> *I will never leave you; I will never forsake you. (Hebrews 13:5, NIV)*

God's Best Timing

Four weeks ago today, I woke up thinking it would be a long hard day for you, for all of us. Two hours after I arrived at the hospital, we were told you were likely going to have open-heart surgery later in the day. Plan B was that you would wait a day for the surgery. A day that would give your body time to rest and give you a day so that you could have your scheduled dialysis.

Or we thought that was the plan.

But as we quickly learned, the Lord had *His own plan* for your healing that Monday afternoon four weeks ago. One that did not involve the best of modern medicine. Or heroics by well-trained physicians and assistants. One that did not involve painful decisions that we as a family would have to make about end of life. In His mercy and love toward you and our family, His plan for healing you came quickly.

God does not have a Plan B.

Four weeks down this painful road, although my heart at times feels as if it has been ripped from my body I can still honestly say *I believe God's timing is always right.* I may not understand it. I may not like it at all. But I believe with every fiber within me that with God there are no accidents. Every incident is intended to bring us closer to Him.

Monday night I went home from the hospital and laid in our bed thinking through everything. The events of the day, how one minute you were kissing me and the next they were telling me you had just died. I thought of our life together, and what would now be my future, *without you.* But mostly I thought of the coming year.

The year of "firsts" that you will not share with us. I found myself thinking that if I could just get through the next 366 days and make it to February 23, 2011. One day past the first year, that I would be good. I would have made it. In that moment, I was willing to settle for "just good."

But in these four weeks, I have realized how ridiculous that thinking is. I will never "*be past you.*" And in the wishing away of the next 365 days, dreading the firsts of everything you will not be a part of and all the important events to come; and just the everyday days when I come home and you are not here . . . regardless of how painful it may be . . . I may miss what God has for me in *His best timing.*

Settling for "just good" would not honor you. It would not honor the Lord who gave His very best, He gave His Son . . . for me. I want God's best for my life and my future life. Recognizing that sometimes it is painful getting there.

Otherwise, all of this would be in vain.

Praise Be to God

Our mailbox continues to be filled with sweet cards of condolence. Today was no different. The following words were written inside one of those cards . . .

> *"Let us continually offer to God our sacrifice of praise" Hebrews 13:15, NIV).*
> *You are a great God.*
> *Your character is holy.*
> *Your truth is absolute.*
> *Your strength is unending.*
> *Your discipline is fair.*
> *Your provisions are abundant for our needs.*
> *Your light is adequate for our path.*
> *Your grace is sufficient for our sins.*
> *You are never early, never late.*
> *You sent your Son in the fullness of time and will return at the consummation of time.*
> *Your plan is perfect.*
> *Bewildering. Puzzling. Troubling.*
> *But perfect.*

We continue to praise our God for His faithfulness during this storm. Just when we think we have made progress in our healing, we take three steps backward. Or we fall backward. I guess that is the "bewildering, puzzling, troubling" part that we do not understand.

Today, looking at the devastation in our hearts, I am not able to grasp how this is perfect and will work for His glory and still for our good.

But we know it to be true. His ways are perfect. I don't just say it. I believe it.

Ali commented earlier today that on the day you died, we were just trying to make it one hour at a time. And how amazing it is that those hours have become days, weeks, and now one month. God has proven His faithfulness time and time again to your family.

Once again, I find myself calling on His all-sufficient grace to make it through the coming day, an hour at a time. Asking that He would be especially near to our children, that He would be tender with them, and that they would feel His presence and know His peace. I continue to praise our God that you are now free from the disease that enslaved your body for thirty-five years. You are healed. You are free.

How can we not praise God for that?

Head vs. Heart

Not a moment too soon. Not a moment too late.

I believe this to be true.

I truly do.

I know that God's word tells me in Psalm 139, "All the days ordained for me were written in your book before one of them came to be."

David says in Psalm 31:15, "My times are in your hands."

We find in Job 14:5, "A person's days are determined; you have decreed the number of his months and have set limits he cannot exceed."

My head knows all of this. My head believes all this to be true. Without question. It's my heart that is having difficulty with this right now.

My heart says *too soon*.

The Last Load of Laundry

You were always so willing to help me here around the house. Because of our opposite work schedules, you were home early in the afternoon and you willingly took on many of the day to day tasks that kept our home running rather smoothly. One of them was you always did your own laundry. You took it on and never seemed to mind doing so.

The last Saturday we spent together, you said you wanted to wait until Sunday after church to do your laundry. We had several things we wanted to do that day, and you had slept so well the night before that you were finally feeling good. So, you decided the laundry could wait until the next day. Of course, the next day we spent in the hospital, and your laundry was never done.

Yesterday I decided it was time to do some laundry. *Your laundry.* I had already sorted it out a couple of weeks ago. Putting it aside not ready to deal with it. But yesterday I felt it was time to wash your clothes that had been in the basket all these weeks.

After I started the first load, I poured dog food in the bowl and went inside. After a while I went to move the clothes into the dryer and start the next load. I found that Darby had turned over the basket and was laying with one of your shirts that she had pulled from the pile . . . don't tell me that dog does not miss you or that she is unaware that something is terribly wrong in her world!

I must admit I am just like Darby. I stood in the garage and smelled your clothes. Taking in every scent I could . . . wanting to memorize it, not wanting to let it go. That's why some of clothes will not be washed or boxed up. My favorite shirts . . . the ones that showed off the freckles on your arms. The ones that made your hair even more beautiful. The suit that you hated but I loved and thought you always looked *"like somebody"* when you wore it is still hanging in the closet, holding the scent of you.

It turned out this was no ordinary laundry day. Yesterday was the last laundry day. There will be no more of your dirty clothes to sort. No more washing and folding, no more matching socks and putting away the clean ones. I had been so concerned about all the firsts that you would miss that I failed to realize that there would also be the lasts that I would have to attend to as well.

From the first to the last, I loved our life together.

I am not trying to paint over anything in these letters, nor am I saying it was always easy. Or that we were always perfectly happy . . . we were imperfect humans . . . but we were perfectly suited for each other. And I loved being your wife and the mother to your four imperfect children. I do believe our lives were perfectly designed to be shared together by a perfectly sovereign God. I loved sharing my life with you.

Even doing the laundry. One last time.

Trail Ride

"Take my yoke upon you and learn from me, for I am gentle and humble in heart, and you will find rest for your souls. For my yoke is easy and my burden is light" (Matthew 11:29–30).

We cannot do this alone. It's not supposed to be easy. If we could . . . if it was, we would have no need for a Savior.

Saturday morning, Mom and I were the only ones at the house. She was sharing something with me that she had read in her devotion time. She used the term "wagon tracks." She told me how God leaves us wagon tracks to follow.

The path will not be smooth or easy, but the way has been made for us. If we follow the tracks, we will get to our destination. But we must follow our Savior.

Even with our large families, it is lonely out here on this trail without you.

What A Wonderful World

We always had this little game we played when we attended an event where there would be dancing. You would ask me to dance. I would say no. You would ask again, and I would hesitate then say yes. I blame my self-conscious nature. I don't feel comfortable on the dance floor. It is what it is.

Saturday night at a family wedding reception when our son tapped me on the shoulder and asked me to dance and I did what came natural to me. I said no. And I immediately saw the hurt in his eyes. He said, *"But I want to dance with my momma."* And my heart melted. Of course, I quickly said yes.

There on the floor with his head buried in my shoulder, he whispered, "I love you so much, Mom." And we both fell apart. Slow dancing to Celine Dion's "Because You Loved Me." Before I knew it, our dance became a group dance/hug with our daughters, our son, and your mother. And then as if on cue, "What A Wonderful World" began to play.

Yes. It is a "wonderful world." You were not there to sing it for us in your best Louis Armstrong voice, so we sang through our tears.

Our hearts are broken . . . but He is the healer of the broken-hearted. God has blessed us so. He is a faithful, loving, sovereign God. His mercies are new every day. We have tested Him and He can be trusted.

It is a wonderful world . . . this is my Father's world. And my world is so much better because you were in it for a season.

This is my Father's world,
and to my listening ears
all nature sings, and round me rings
the music of the spheres.
This is my Father's world:
I rest me in the thought
of rocks and trees, of skies and seas;
his hand the wonders wrought.
This is my Father's world,
the birds their carols raise,
the morning light, the lily white,
declare their maker's praise.
This is my Father's world:
he shines in all that's fair;
in the rustling grass I hear him pass;
he speaks to me everywhere.
This is my Father's world.
O let me ne'er forget
that though the wrong seems oft so strong,
God is the ruler yet.
This is my Father's world:
why should my heart be sad?
The Lord is King; let the heavens ring!
God reigns; let the earth be glad!
(This Is My Father's World, Maltbie Davenport
Babcock, Composer, 1901)

A Beautiful Sight

It had been your desire to be an organ donor and offer a second chance at life to another family. But due to your kidney disease and months of dialysis, along with years of medication and your heart attack, you did not qualify to offer that gift.

However, you helped restore sight to individuals with tissue donation through The Alabama Eye Bank. They tell me that tissue donation benefits others in many ways: it can be used for sight-restoring transplant surgery, to help medical professionals enhance their knowledge and skills, or used by researchers in advancing their understanding of currently incurable eye diseases.

Obviously, these uses benefit visually impaired people and their families. Just as we were hoping to be on the receiving end of a kidney transplant one day . . . I know that you would be so happy in learning that you could help bring the gift of sight to others. Our family is rejoicing that two individuals have received a very special gift of sight from you, our very special man. I am so proud that even in death you could help make the life of someone else happier. Easier. Sighted. Amazing.

You had beautiful eyes. They were hidden behind your glasses. But they were there. What a wonderful thought this morning that when Christ returns and all His elect are gathered together with Him, I will see you and those beautiful eyes again, your body whole and well.

And I will join you in singing praise to the Lord. What a beautiful sight that will be!

I miss seeing you.

raw

this morning the reality is just too raw.
and again, i was thinking i had made all this . . . little, bitty . . .
progress.
when i am asked how am i doing, i just smile.
but what i want to scream is this just sucks!
my eyes are burning.
our kids are heartbroken.
our dog is sad.
i roll over in our bed and your side is cold and undisturbed.
when will i start sleeping all night again?
i am so tired . . .
i miss you so.

White Picket Fence

Like a lightning bolt it occurred to me that during grieving your death, I am also grieving that white picket fence life I dreamed of when I was younger.

The one I would close my eyes and pretend to be in when I would use my hairbrush microphone and sing "I Honestly Love You" with Debbie Boone on the radio.

We had a great life together. Yes, we had our bumps in the road leading up to the fence. And when you got to the fence, there were places that needed a new coat of paint. But once inside, past the gate there was love.

Goofy . . . love.

I dare anyone beyond the gate to hurt you . . . love.

Good . . . love.

You drive me crazy . . . love.

My one and only . . . love.

I cannot for the life of me figure you out . . . love.

Run away with me . . . love.

Who the heck are you . . . love.

You are mine . . . love.

It has been worth it all . . . love. *I Honestly Love You* . . . love.

You Remain

It is amazing how much of you remains here with us.

When I look across the table at Andrew or Ali and without effort or thought, they each wink at me with their left eye . . . I see you.

In April's love of music . . . you are there.

Amy's quick sense of humor and laughter fills the room . . . just like yours.

You have passed to our children your work ethic. Your fierce sense of loyalty to family. A caring and compassionate spirit. So much of you remains here, within our children. What a blessing.

Lighting My Path

Your word is a lamp to my feet. And a light to my path. (Psalm 119:105)

For the commandment is a lamp and the teaching is light; And reproofs for discipline are the way of life. (Proverbs 6:23, ESV)

You always had a flashlight. In all shapes and sizes. Colors and types. For some reason you seemed to be fascinated by flashlights.

I remember when we were first married and we lived on the farm in New Hope, you took one of those huge spotlights and mounted it to the front of your truck. You would go out in the fields late at night and shine that light on unsuspecting animals or trespassers up to no good.

That thing was so powerful it would shine through the thickest fog. I remember riding along with you and wondering if we would be able to find our way home through the deep fog. But the spotlight always did its job.

Your word is a lamp to my feet. And a light to my path. God has provided a light for us to navigate our way safely through the fog of life. His word is a comfort during this time. A lamp to my feet . . . a light to my path.

However, I do think it's funny that I can't find a working flashlight in our house!

There Is Good

Lost in the marking of time since you died is the one-year anniversary of your first fistula placement. It seems so long ago in so many ways. And in other ways it seems like just yesterday that we were sitting there in the surgery waiting area, not sure what to expect. But clinging to the hope that the port would not be used for a while . . . eighteen months at least. But it was not to be. And we know how that all played out.

I guess I am still looking for a reason to say that He is not sovereign. That He is not good. Not trustworthy or faithful.

I am still looking for a reason to say that because my dreams have been shattered and my plans thwarted that it changes who He is. Because I sleep three hours at best, and spend my days fighting daydreams of you that He is unloving . . . unkind.

But I can't.

Because He has met every need. Understands every cry for help. Is there in the dark of night when I cannot sleep. Is trustworthy and faithful. Loving and kind. Merciful and true.

His ways are not man's ways . . . indeed they are not. His timetable is not set by things of this earth but rather by His good pleasure and what will bring Him the most glory. I have said over and over that He is using your death for His glory and my good. I wanted desperately for it to be some other way. For His glory to come through some other means. For my good to be accomplished in a less hurtful fashion.

I do not understand it. But I believe it to be true, He is working good in my life.

During all this pain, there is still so much good. So much to praise Him for. I just never knew that praising Him could be so costly or so painful.

Psalm 68:19

"Blessed be the Lord, who daily bears us up. God is our salvation" (ESV).

He is still God. It has been three months.

I never thought I would have made it this far . . . this long. I have had no choice really. Over and over I continue to ask how those who do not believe in Jesus can face times such as this. Where do they find hope outside of Him?

There are days that it has been like a Band-Aid being carelessly ripped off a wound. As if I am processing everything for the first time. The dread . . . the pit in my stomach because I know what is inevitably coming. Just like when it was report card day in junior high and I was summoned to Dad's home office and the yellow office chair. I always got sick on report card day . . . honestly, I have spent many days these last three months being a little sick.

But at the center of it all, we are finding the faithfulness of the Lord. Repeatedly. His faithfulness does not change the fact that we hurt so deeply or that we wish it was some other way. But in the pain, His faithfulness gives us hope.

He is still God. He does not change. His love for us is the same. Everyday.

Our hearts miss you so much. But God is soothing our hurts, bearing our burdens. He is a big God. And we continue to praise Him . . .

Amputation

I recently started reading *A Grief Observed*[13] by C.S. Lewis. The forward written by Madeleine L 'Engle has shaken me to my core each time I have gone back to reread it. She says the following:

> *The death of a beloved is an amputation . . .*
> *when two people marry, each one has to accept that*
> *one of them will die before the other.*

Oh, my goodness! I have been searching for the words to describe what I have been feeling. With no disrespect to anyone who has experienced the physical loss of a limb, this is exactly what I feel has happened to me.

There are days when I feel as if my hand is missing. Other days when I feel it is my entire right side that is gone . . . dependent on how deeply the pain is in that moment. One thing is for sure, my heart has been ripped out and put back in time and again. Over and over.

I know He is working all things for my good. I am trying so hard to trust Him. But this is just so not fun. You are my better half. I don't like that you have been amputated from me.

---

13 CS Lewis, *A Grief Observed*, Harper One (2009)

The Comforter

A result of being called to walk this road God has called me to walk in is the encouragement and love I have received from our family and friends through e-mails, phone calls, texts, and many other communications. I checked my e-mail before I went to bed, and there was a sweet message of encouragement:

> *You are loved, Dana . . . I was listening to a message from Warren Weirsbe yesterday, and he was talking about the names of the Holy Spirit—one of the names as we know is "Comforter." He said that comforter was not the soft, cushy kind of helper we sometimes imagine, but Comfort means "with fortification!" I thought that was neat—He comes to fortify and strengthen us in our need—what a COMFORT! Weirsbe said the unchristian can't understand this, but I promise I thought right as he was speaking "Dana knows . . ."*

I DO KNOW.

I think that at first I needed that soft, cushy kind of tender comfort. In those first weeks, that is what got me through. But in these last weeks, it is the fortifying, sustaining, strengthening comfort that Warren Weirsbe is speaking of. That comfort is what I have needed. That comfort is what He has provided.

And I know, that I know, that I know that He will continue to provide what I need. Even when I cannot see it. Even when I cannot feel it. Even when the tears cloud my vision. Even when the hurt is so deep I think I cannot continue.

The Comforter has come.

He Is with Me

On February 25th, the day we buried you, I wrote the following:

> *I can listen to that voice of doubt whispering in my ear "where was your God four days ago?", "how could your loving God allow you to hurt this way?", or I can cling to the truth that I know. I do have a* hope *in Him. He* is working *for my good, even when I cannot see it or feel it just yet. Even when it does not make sense to me. When my heart is so broken, I think I cannot possibly go on. When I look into the faces of those I love so dearly and I cannot heal their unspeakable pain. The only comfort I can offer them is . . . Jesus is real. God's word is true. And despite our earthly circumstances that seem to contradict, I know that He is a good and sovereign God who can be trusted.*

I am constantly being given encouragement by our sweet friends. A note was left in our mailbox yesterday with a photocopy of a devotion. I do not know where it came from, so I cannot give it proper credit, but the following words spoke to my heart:

> *We need to realize a profound truth in the midst of our sadness: God is in it. We may find that hard to believe. How could a loving God allow this disaster to strike us? But the witness of the Word is*

that God is sovereign and He is intimately involved in our pain. He was with Joseph in his brother's treachery and his long imprisonment; He was with Joshua in every battle for the Promised Land; He was with Jeremiah in the destruction of Jerusalem; and He was actually in Jesus on the Cross. His hand had a purpose in every one of these traumatic events. He did not frantically come up with plans B, C, or D because of an unforeseen failure in His plan A. He has already counted on the trials to come.

He was with each of them. He is with me.

I am not promised an easy resolution. This gut-wrenching pain is deep and real. I will not heal quickly.

Quickly healing is not how God has purposed this.

> *"Just because life seems difficult does not mean God has missed something. He knows all about difficult. He did not promise the easy, pain-free life. He promised redemption."*

And He promised . . .

> *"I am with you always, even to the end of the age" (Matthew 28:20, ESV).*

I Hate Death

The light bulb did not just come on. I have known this since day one. But the truth is . . . I hate death. I hate everything about it.

It is so final. *In this life, anyway.*

This sounds so silly to say because your situation has not suddenly changed . . . but I feel you slipping away from me more and more every day. Although you are everywhere I look in our home—in the personalities of our children, in their eyes, in the memories I have of you when I look at photographs, in the retelling of favorite stories—you are there . . . so clear. Crystal clear.

I open the closet and I can still smell you on your clothes. The last valentine you gave me is on the dresser. Your wallet, keys, and cell phone are in a basket on the bedside table. I'm using your Bible at church now.

The separation of death stings so very bad. The tidal wave of emotions is nauseating. Looking at photos, reading a valentine, smelling your clothes, or holding your Bible do not make up for the fact that you are not here. And every day that passes, you are farther away from me than you were yesterday.

I know that I could reverse that thought and say that I am one day closer to seeing you . . . but today, this day it does not help. It just hurts. I hate death. I hate the way it separates. The way it stings.

Every Day Is Hard

Death continues to be a constant in my life. Almost as if to be laughing at me. Everywhere I turn.

I went to the funeral home for a visitation this afternoon. I tried my best to stay in the room with the family and our friends. But I looked up and found that I was as far across the room from everyone . . . and the casket . . . as was humanly possible. Still in the room, yet not.

Friends kept asking, "Isn't this hard for you . . . going to a funeral home?" Again, I responded that every day is hard. Some days harder than others. But I must keep on living life, anything less would be unhealthy.

But still . . .

- Waking up alone, going to sleep alone . . . *hard.*
  After all the years we were married, you just get used to having somebody in the bed with you. I miss you being there.
- Going to church . . . *hard.*
  Oh my gosh, we keep singing songs that make it difficult to worship without crying.
- Family functions . . . *hard.*
  I have concluded that you were the life's blood of our family! Everything revolved around you . . . in a good way. Your laughter. Your humor. Your helpfulness. Your silliness. Your talents. And your absence is screaming at us.
- Making decisions . . . *hard.*

I have said it before . . . you were so good at *letting me think I was in charge.* Now that I have the final word in our house, I don't want it. I loved the comfort of knowing that you knew best. And that you would do the right thing after I had my last word . . . I don't like having the last word so much anymore.

•   Living a new life . . . *hard.*

Okay really . . . does this need an explanation? Right now, this new thing that I am doing just sucks without you.

I did not write any of the following, but took it all from John Piper's *Desiring God Blog:*

> *Death itself is a devastating and horrible thing. But God promises to work all things—including death—for good for those who love him and are called by him. (Romans 8:28)*
>
> *Isaiah 57:1–2, ESV gives us one glimpse into how God views the death of his saints:*
>
> *The righteous man perishes, and no one lays it to heart; devout men are taken away, while no one understands. For the righteous man is taken away from calamity; he enters into peace; they rest in their beds who walk in their uprightness.*
>
> *"In this world [we] will have tribulation" (John 16:33ESV). We will only stop having tribulation when God takes us home.*
>
> *The Lord Jesus finally sees his great desire for us fulfilled: "Father, I desire that they also, whom you have given me, may be with me where I am, to see my glory" (John 17:24, ESV).*
>
> *Which is why "precious in the sight of the Lord is the death of his saints" (Psalm 116:15, ESV).*

Even though this is hard and devastating and horrible, I know that He is making something good out of this for me. I know that

He is not wasting this moment on me. And that He will bring about His glory in some way through this. And so, I will continue to praise Him . . . even when it is hard to do so.

I am so thankful that you are there . . . in His sight. I don't understand all the mysteries involved in it. But I do understand the words *"peace and rest,"* and there is comfort in knowing that *you are experiencing those right now.*

What a merciful and faithful Savior to love me over and over when I doubt and question one day. Then am so sure and strong the next. Only to fall on my face in fear and anguish the next.

Every day is hard. Again, I must ask . . . how do people do this without a Savior?

I cannot believe how much this hurts.

Photographs and Memories

We live life as if it were a motion picture. Loss turns life into a snapshot. The movement stops; everything freezes. We find ourselves looking at picture albums to remember the motion picture of our lives that once was but can no longer be. Loss takes what we might do and turns it into what we can never do.

Loss freezes life into a snapshot. We are stuck with what was instead of what could have been. (Jerry Sittser, A Grace Disguised)

We have been looking at a ton of photographs lately. Going through albums and shoe boxes. It has been a fun experience—relieving moments that I had forgotten about. *Some things I wish I could forget.* Embarrassing photos I hope no one outside our family sees. We have laughed at ourselves. And at you.

You are such a funny man.

But here's the deal. It's one thing to sit and look at a photo and think how cute our babies were at any given age. Or how much fun we had at an Auburn game. Laughing at a funny expression on your face. Or trying to name Big Daddy's farm dogs. But to think about the background story that was going on before the photo was taken sheds a whole new light on the picture.

We were invited to a Christmas dinner in 1999. We almost didn't go. There was anger and bitterness in our home. We were both wrong. Too stubborn to admit it and forgive each other as we should have days earlier and it snowballed. We had barely spoken to each other in four days. That night, we only communicated enough to make the decision to attend this function rather than stay home together. So we showed up and played the part of the happy couple that everyone expected us to be. We were both so incredibly miserable. But, somehow, we managed to fake our best smile.

I am still reading . . . very slowly . . . *A Grace Disguised*[14] by Jerry Sittser.

I like what he says about his relationship with his wife: "*We loved each other well, though imperfectly. We were building a meaningful life together. We were becoming something better, but the relationship had not yet matured to what it could have been.*"

In reliving the memories of our life together through words and photographs, I think it's important for me to remember that while *today* it seems that we were perfect . . . oh my goodness . . . we were so far from it. Now looking back to that night, we were so fired up angry about something so trivial that I cannot even believe we wasted four days of our lives being angry over it. However, I am sure you secretly enjoyed being "punished by my silence."

At the time of your death we had grown up a little. We had weathered some major storms in our family, and our relationship and come out of them for the better. We had matured in our communication skills. We were also in a place where you and I were loving each other well. Our children were all grown and responsible for themselves. The distraction of raising a family no longer took away from building our relationship. We were more attentive to each other, we were better together than we ever had been. Some people call it more spiritual. I am not so sure I like that term, but I understand what they mean.

But unlike Mary Poppins, we were still practically imperfect in every way. Thankfully, Jesus came to save those who are imperfect and in need of a Savior. Although we are imperfect, He loves perfectly; and through Him life has meaning and purpose.

---

[14] Jerry Sittser, *A Grace Disguised: How the Soul Grows Through Loss Zondervan*, Expanded Edition (December 2004)

Flowers

This morning, I rolled over and looked at the clock. It was 1:32 a.m.

I was at The Embassy Suites in Franklin, Tennessee, in a bed alone on our thirtieth anniversary. Not exactly the way I had dreamed it would be when I was a blushing bride.

I was not totally alone. Our kids were with me. But my heart was heavy. I was trying not to cry again. I have spent so many days crying. But it's odd the things that go through your mind when you wake up so early on your thirtieth anniversary and your husband is not there and everyone else is sleeping soundly.

"Do you even celebrate your anniversary after your husband is dead . . . is this what it feels like to lose your mind . . . I should have had the oil changed before I left home."

You were predictably unpredictable. Nine times out of ten I knew what you would say and do. But that tenth time, you sure knew how to surprise me.

For twenty-nine years, you had flowers delivered for our anniversary. We never were big on gifts; we just never have gone down that road. Except for the one year you gave me a vacuum cleaner for my birthday, and I threw a fit like a four-year-old. Then three months later, you surprised me with a ring you had a friend of ours make. It has your birthstone in it. That's why the ring is so special. It was so out of character for you to buy it for me.

I laid there this morning, and it hit me like a ton of bricks that flowers would no longer be delivered. It was not the worst news I have ever processed. But it was just one more thing. An ending to another part of our history and way we did things that will never be the same.

We had an emotional ride home this afternoon. Poor April, she was unsure what to do with me other than rub my back with one hand and steer the car with the other.

But when we got home, three floral arrangements were sitting on our front porch. Friends and family knew that celebrating the first Father's Day and our thirtieth anniversary without you would be difficult.

We are constantly loved beyond what I can fathom. There are so many reminders that we are not alone. Even when I wake up in the dark and you are not next to me. There is a sweet fragrance in the air, inside our home, and waiting on our front porch.

Max Lucado says, "God's lights in our dark nights are as numerous as the stars; if only we'll look for them."[15]

Looking for those stars and smelling the flowers along the way.

I am missing you so very much.

---

[15] Max Lucado, *Grace for the Moment*

First Place

I remember when I was little and we got our first color television. We were so excited the day Daddy brought it through the door. I remember asking if we were *"the first people in the world to own one"*—always wanting to be the first to do something.

I was the first of my friends to marry. Choosing you and starting a family over college sorority parties. I have never regretted my decision to stay home. Although there have been times when I know a formal education would have been beneficial, but a life education is just as meaningful.

On the day of your memorial service, three different people reminded me that I was a young widow. I hate that word and still recoil at the thought of it being attached to me. But in conversation, it was noted that I was the first one from our childhood and our close circle of friends to bury a spouse.

Again, the first.

It's lonely being in first place. There are so many people who will tell you they "understand how you *must* feel." But they don't. Because they have never been where I am. I am forty-nine years old. You were fifty-one. Our children were grown. We had plans. *This was not supposed to be happening now.*

I know plenty of people who have buried their spouse. They are my parents' age. Or they were at a different stage in life when their spouses died. I cannot name one other friend my age who is where I am today. I feel like I am out here all by myself, it's lonely being in first place.

I miss you so much.

Flickering Flames

I have begun to read a devotional at night, *Grace for the Moment* by Max Lucado. Last night I was reading about how we are often guilty of thinking that God can only be seen in big ways—that miracles only happen if they are earth shattering, or *unbelievable*.

"Because we look for the bonfire we miss the candle. Because we listen for the shout we miss the whisper. But it is in burnished candles that God comes, and through whispered promises He speaks; 'When you doubt, look around: I am closer than you think.'"

I am so guilty of wanting the big bonfire. Or the writing in the sky. But I think He is gently whispering to me, "Even though you feel alone out there, be of good cheer! My way is perfect. You are greatly loved. You are made in my image."

This will not be a quick fix. It will not be easy. But He promises me, *"For I am the LORD, your God, who takes hold of your right hand and says to you, do not fear, I will help you" (Isaiah 41:13).*

If I fail to trim the wick down before I burn the candle, the room will get all smoke-filled when I blow it out. Then the beautiful scent from the candle gets lost in the smell of the smoke. The sweet fragrance is gone.

I have become so easily distracted and discouraged lately. I have taken my eyes off Christ. Caught looking for bonfires and listening for shouts. When really, I should have been looking for flickering flames and listening for whispers. I have completely missed the smell of His sweet fragrance . . . *which is in abundance.*

This process is not for the faint of heart or those who think they have it all together. Many days I wake up and go *"oh yeah, this really is true.* "And it's all fresh news that must be processed again throughout the day. Other days I just pick up where I left off when I went to sleep the night before. I feel as if I am constantly riding a tidal wave of emotions still, never knowing when the next storm will blow in. And that makes it easy to miss the sweet smell of the Lord because of the distraction and tension I feel. Always afraid of what my reactions will be to a situation. Songs at church (I had no idea how difficult it would be to go to church without you). Random conversations with people. Questions asked . . . I am beginning to hate all the questions that are being asked of me.

I want big miracles in my progress toward healing! *Not flickers of flames . . .*

I want the smell of five dozen roses. *Not one single rose.* I want to hear the song live and in person. *Not a whisper in a storm.*

Oh, dear God, help my anxious, unbelieving, impatient heart today!

Unwelcome Guest

I have been living with a guest in our home—an uninvited and most unwelcome guest. This guest has just walked in and plopped down, became too comfortable, and will not leave. I thought maybe my guest had left a few weeks ago. *Really? What was I thinking?* But it appears that is not the case.

My guest is grief. Apparently, grief takes day trips and then comes in late at night. But then there are times when I am in the car alone, and grief pops up from behind me. But grief's favorite time to show up is when I have been out of town and am headed home. Grief knows I am especially vulnerable then, because you are not there on the porch with Darby waiting on me. It seems to me that is the time grief taunts me the most. So I'm thinking that I will not ever go anywhere and spend the night away from home again. Because I seem to be doing a lot of coming and going lately.

Which of course I know is so stupid. *Of course,* I will go out of town again. But in the moment, driving home with tears running down my face I tell myself, *I will never do this again.*

I have always enjoyed having friends and family in our home. I think I am a very welcoming person. Unfortunately, from everything I read and everything I hear, grief is setting up a tent and sticking around for a while. Grief also checks in and out at will. I can't just serve up a chicken casserole and send him on his way.

I know that eventually life will get better, that the good days will run together and there will be less of the sad days. But I also know that it will take time. I realize that grieving you is the cost of loving you. But right now, this unwelcome guest is here.

Grief weighs a ton, and grief sometimes makes it hard to breathe.

And when I say *"I'm okay"* or *"I'm hanging in there"* . . . I'm not telling the truth. I'm just pretending our house is empty and the unwelcome guest has paid the bill, checked out, moved on down the road.

Unshakable Faith

I had no trouble believing God's word is true on Day 1 or 15 or 30. But after four months when the rest of the world has gone back to their normal life, I am having a hard time believing. When our lives will never be normal again. I know all the right words to say. I believe all the truths of the Gospel and would stake my life on them. But somehow in these last few days, *I don't feel they are true.*

Is this a crisis of faith . . . or is it just a crisis?

I stayed in bed until three thirty yesterday. Just lying there, staring at the ceiling or buried under the covers with my phone off. I never even checked my e-mail or the calls at my office. I keep saying I feel as if I am being smothered. But then when I'm left alone, I fold up in a cocoon. I am sure there are those who feel helpless as to how or what to do for me. I know I probably appear stand-offish and cold, not wanting to engage in meaningful conversation, or any conversation at all. I feel desperate to keep things very light, not wanting to get into deep discussions about life and death, or *"how are you really doing?"* (insert the head tilt and the sad half-smile that says, I am so glad this is not happening to me).

In the past when I've had surgery, I have always thought it was so wonderful to go to sleep and wake up several hours later when all the business was taken care of. The surgeon did his magic, and I was totally unaware of what was going on. I woke up better off for having been there. I feel like I had a surgical procedure four months ago, without anesthesia. Maybe just some topical numbing medicine that has been slowly wearing off and now the full force of the pain has set in.

There is no prescription available except to just live through the pain. I would have preferred the anesthesia option. I know in the long run I would eventually still have to deal with the pain, but today it seems the best choice. I would have chosen to not have any "surgery" at all and still have you here with me for another thirty years. But I was not consulted before my procedure.

I had no idea that loving you would be so painful. But I would do it all again. Dear God, help me choose hope. Help me choose faith. Help me choose life. Give me an unshakable faith in You.

Out of Order

It used to infuriate me to watch you be so incredibly inpatient with the cable company when the Internet or cable would be down. Or if there was a power outage in our neighborhood and we were without electricity. You always thought it was effective to call more than once, or four times, to report the loss of service. You were always the squeaky wheel. But I don't think our services were restored all that much faster. You just seemed to huff and puff and stomp all over the house that much more.

I like order. I like for things to be in a certain place. I don't like chaos. There are those who function best under pressure. I am not that person. The roller-coaster of emotions that I feel these days offers me no semblance of order. The things I am feeling are completely unpredictable. Something that yesterday would bring me to tears . . . today I may laugh about. But other days, like today, I can hardly think your name without my knees buckling.

This is complete madness! I feel like I am in the den after six hours of no electricity and all the windows are painted shut. Covered in sweat. Waiting on the utility company to show up. Sitting here with just the one little candle glowing in the darkness.

The candle is Jesus's promise of comfort and blessing to those who go through the process of grief and mourning. *"Blessed are those who mourn, for they will be comforted"* (Matthew 5:4).

In the chaos, in the madness, in the middle of the emotional disorder that I am feeling, even in the doubt that I am experiencing, I am clinging to His promise that He will comfort me. He has not failed me. His word is true.

I may be out of order . . . but He is not.

The Puzzle

We did not do it every year, but for several years we attempted to put together a puzzle during the holidays. It was always one with a beautiful detailed scene. We would open the box at Thanksgiving and work on it all throughout the holiday season. If we were successful, it would be completed before the big crystal ball dropped in Times Square on December 31st.

To make it *"more fun,"* we would choose a puzzle with 1000 or 1500 pieces so that it would take the entire season to complete. It was always a fun Thanksgiving weekend. But as time and schedules demanded, our attention to the puzzle was neglected. It became difficult to ensure that all the pieces were accounted for when days and even weeks would go by and no progress was made toward completion. Eventually, in frustration when yet another Christmas tradition had seen better days, I would box up the unfinished puzzle and toss it in the hall closet until the next year. Or never . . . if we purchased a new puzzle and attempted the whole process in vain again.

Our family is much like the Christmas puzzle. We are a work in progress. There are many pieces to who we are. Sometimes our six pieces would fit together perfectly, without work or effort. Other times our pieces must be forced into place because they were cut into odd shapes, and although they fit together, sometimes they did not fit together as easily as others.

Our puzzle is missing a piece. It was not left in the box as all the pieces were dumped onto the table. It was not accidently knocked onto the floor. The landscape of our beautiful scenery has been forever changed. Our children have never experienced life without a father, just as I have never experienced life without you, a wife without her husband.

Your death has not been convenient or pain-free for any of us.

In his book *When Life is Changed Forever*,[16] Rick Taylor says the following:

> *Death is separation. A tearing apart of that which is united and one. We are hurt by death because it tears apart something good and right, something natural and normal, without respect to families or friends.*
>
> *The author of Hebrews wrote that people should fix their eyes on Jesus, the Author and Finisher of their faith so that they would not grow weary and lose heart. Jesus, the true God, will not let you down but will keep you strong in your time of distress, that is what you need. Someone who will be there for you. A God who can make a difference.*

---

[16] Rick Taylor, *When Life Changed Forever*, Harvest House Publishers, January 1993.

One Year Ago

One year. I started writing to you one year ago today.

There were some days when I did not write. Other days when I wrote more than once. I never thought I would stick with it. I didn't realize I had so much to say. Never knew we would be taken down this road.

Yet, here I am.

In the last few days, I have gone back and read every one of the letters.

I have read things that I cannot believe I wrote. Begged myself to push "delete" and erase letters from the memory banks. Embarrassed that I shared so much. But those were my thoughts. My heart at that moment in time. It would be cheating to change history at this point. So I will leave what has been said and hope the reader understands.

If not . . . do I care?

You lived to Day 214 of writing letters and on Day 215, I stopped numbering them. Instead counting them for a different reason. You never posted a comment on the blog. We just talked about them each day. You never asked me to change anything I wrote. You laughed with me and cried with me. And once I made the public proclamation that I would rub lotion on your feet, you made me live up to it. *Even if I was mad at you.* When I bragged about your smoking and grilling skills, you were especially proud. You encouraged me to keep it real and honest and not gloss over any aspect of our life. We are very real people, living a very real life, dying a very real death. It has not always been pretty. But it has been ours . . . therefore it has been beautiful.

I am not sure why I have opened our personal life and now my grief to such a public display. It makes no sense especially given the fact that I am one who guards my privacy with a passion. Truthfully, I despise it when I hear that matters of my life are being discussed by others. *So why have I done this?* It would have been much easier if I had only shared all this with you privately. Many days I wish I had done exactly that.

Change

Looking back on the last five months, I feel as if I have been treated like this fragile woman of sorts. I think it has happened naturally. No one is to blame. So many who are so closely involved in my life have never experienced death so personally or from such a deep perspective. So the instinct is to love much and often. And to allow it to happen.

Career wise I have barely shown up since Monday, February 22. I have kept my scheduled appointments after taking two weeks off. But I have not given 100 percent of my professional self. I have just been in the office. Made phone calls and handled claims. Talked to my daddy and cried. And cried. I am blessed with the ability to come and go as I please because I work for me and set my schedule. If I was required to work a forty-hour week and punch-a-time clock, I probably would have been fired long before now. In most companies, I would have been given three days to bury you, handle all the business, and then return to work.

The last two weeks, I have seen a distinct change in my heart and my attitude. I don't know if it is simply getting over a hump emotionally so to speak. Or if it is because I have been given an opportunity with work that offers a challenge and it's something new and different. Or if it is just the place I am in the healing process. Maybe it's all of these working in concert. I know I would not have been ready for any of this three months ago.

I still wish you were here. I wish it every day. And every night.

Oh sing to the LORD a new song; sing to the LORD, all the earth! Sing to the LORD, bless his name; tell of his salvation from day to day. Declare his glory among the nations, his marvelous works among all the peoples! For great is the LORD, and greatly to be praised; he is to be feared above all gods. (Psalm 96, ESV)

Scars

You were my first thought this morning. Just as you have been every morning. I wake up thinking, *Yes, all of this is still true.* I wonder how long I will do this, how long I will replay the events of that day . . . that week. When will it no longer be necessary to relive that time in order to carry on with my day?

When Amy graduated from college in May 2005, we were all so excited. The night before graduation, I was in her dorm room and noticed that her graduation gown was wrinkled, so I took it down the hall to the laundry room and began to iron it. Somehow the iron slipped and burned my wrist. For weeks I dealt with that burn. It eventually left a long scar on my wrist that is a constant reminder of Amy's graduation day. It has become to me a testimony of the sacrifices made during that period of our life for our daughter to attend college and all that she accomplished.

Yesterday I was talking to Momma and was telling her that I feel like the grieving process is like a scab that is healing, but once you get in the shower it softens and washes off. The injury becomes exposed and must scab over again. Then you shower and the process starts all over again. But each time the scab gets smaller and smaller until there is only a reminder of the pain that caused the scar. It no longer hurts physically. But the emotional pain is there.

I think everyone carries those types of scars, whether they are visible or not. And as Mom said in our conversation yesterday, if we could ever get to the place where we just say, "Lord you have put me here. I don't understand why. But I trust you. Please teach me what you have for me to learn and use me for your glory." If we ever totally surrender to Him in that way, when we see the scars in our life, we would see them through tears of thankfulness rather than remembering the pain that they brought into our lives.

The pain is not so fresh anymore. When the Band-Aid is carefully removed from the wound, it's not as big. But there are days when it gets ripped off unintentionally. Your death will leave a big scar. There will always be constant reminders of our life together. But we have a big God, and I am trusting that He will one day heal the wound.

"Commit your way to the LORD, trust him,
and he will act" (Psalm 37:5, ESV).

Play That Funky Music

It is hard enough just to go to church *without you*. It would have been so much easier if you had requested that we sing something by Lynard Skynard or Queen at your graveside service, rather than "Be Thou My Vision." We sang it again today.

I really do wish we would start singing "Freebird" or "Play That Funky Music" occasionally. Until then, I guess I must again take comfort in the words to one of your favorites.

> Be Thou my vision, O Lord of my heart
> Naught be all else to me, save that Thou art
> Thou my best thought by day or by night
> Waking or sleeping Thy presence my light
> Be thou my wisdom and Thou my true word
> I ever with Thee and Thou with me, Lord
> Thou my great Father, I, thy true son
> Thou in me dwelling and I with Thee one
> Riches I heed not nor man's empty praise
> Thou mine inheritance now and always
> Thou and thou only first in my heart
> High King of heaven my treasure Thou art
> High King of heaven my victory won

May I reach heaven's joys, O bright heaven's Sun
Heart of my own heart whatever befall
Still be my vision O Ruler of all[17]

Your library of favorite music was odd.
But then you, my funky white boy, were also very odd.

---

[17] "Be Thou My Vision," Eleanor Hull 1912

August 16, 2010

See, I am doing a new thing! Now it springs up; do you not perceive it? I am making a way in the desert and streams in the wasteland.
—*Isaiah 43:19*

Another Monday.

One hundred and seventy-five days. Almost six months now.

All these markers of time since I held your hand and heard you laugh. No one bothered to tell you that people hooked up to all those monitors in the CICU were not supposed to be laughing and smiling just mere minutes before the end of their life. I am thankful for that.

On the Monday that you died, I listened to the stirring in my heart and soul and left the room without any prompting from the nurse or doctor. Our goodbye was a very good one. Thinking you were preparing for surgery, we could say some things that needed to be said—words that my heart can still hear. We did not know what was soon to be, but I know the Lord orchestrated our time together as well as the events of the day.

For the past six months, I have continued to openly share our life.

I have been as honest as I know how to be. I have shared pieces of our past, our present, and talked about what my future now looks like without you. Writing about our life, your death, and what God is teaching me through this season of grief has been healing to me.

But where there is healing, there must first be pain.

In walking with the Lord, we are taken places we never intended to go. He leads us to places we often do not want to follow. He shapes, grows, molds, and directs us in ways that are uncomfortable. We find we can be stretched beyond what we never imagined was possible. When we question Him; if there are answers, we do not always understand them. If there is silence, we doubt His love. Yet, He remains the same. He never leaves us. He is always there.

I now sense that He is leading me on a new and different journey in this process that is called grief. I have no idea where He is taking me or what there is still to learn about Him or myself. But I do know that He asks for a heart of trust and obedience. I have struggled with this for some time now. I thought it was settled weeks ago.

Apparently, it was not.

I have come to a place on this journey through grief where I feel that to keep moving forward I must listen once again to that voice in my heart telling me that it is time to go. It is time to allow the Lord to teach me and heal me *privately*. Not so that I can *move on* or *get over you*. But so that I can lean into His tenderness and gentle care. I want to experience the fullness of life that He intended for me to experience *in Him*. And I am realizing that I can't do any of that if I continue to live this grief so openly.

Things I Miss

Several weeks ago, I took a break from writing to you. What had been healing suddenly became too hard. I had to stop. I needed to not deal with the reality of your absence. But tonight, I find that I am so lonely, and the only thing I can think to do is write to you again. There are so many things that I miss about you, about us, our life together.

I miss the intimate things. The way you would pull me into you when I came home from work. Refusing to let me just kiss you and walk away. The holding of hands, linking our fingers.

How you would brush my hair off my face and smile at me when I was trying to argue with you. A wink. That random slap on my bottom when I was at the kitchen sink and you would pass by. Having my tears wiped away by the only man I have ever loved. Knowing that I was yours. And you were mine. The feeling of total security. Freedom to sleep with abandon knowing you would protect me.

The meaning behind the laugh that no one else understood. The eye contact. Raised eyebrows. Again, that wink that melted my heart every time.

The hugs. You hugged so tight and so good. The conversation that made up who we were. The "we" that few people knew. I miss all of it and so much more.

I miss you. I miss us.

December 29, 2010

I have spent the last few weeks (months) rereading what I have written over the last eighteen months. It has once again left me unable to write much until today. I would start to write and then realize that for my mental healing to continue, I needed to stop. It had become too emotional for me.

We have made it to the point I had been dreading since the night I crawled into bed after you died. We made it through the holidays and then your birthday. For some reason, I thought we would fall apart and not do well. I guess I underestimated how well we have stuck together as a family, how well we have healed, how well we have allowed our friends to love us.

I underestimated God and His tender mercy and faithful love. I have talked about it for ten months now. But I guess I thought He would not come through during these most painful of days . . . when everyone else was celebrating and we were hurting the most. But once again, He did not fail us. Of course, our celebration was bittersweet, but it was a good time of celebrating and remembering.

We are each moving forward with His help. We are learning to be happy. And I am thankful for all that our past represents and all that I have in the future before me because of the life I shared with you.

I love you. So very much.

January 2, 2011

I marked every Monday in my 2010 day planner to indicate the number of days since you told me goodbye. Likewise, I also marked the weeks on those Mondays as well. For some reason, it seemed important for me to know how many weeks it had been when I looked at my calendar. I stopped marking after your birthday, which was the last Monday of the year. Choosing not to continue the counting in 2011.

It seems rather pointless. In my grief recovery class, they indicated this was a common practice. But I am wondering why does it matter how many Mondays since you have been gone. How does it help me to know that tomorrow will be week 44 or is it 43? Day 317 or day 318. It is not as if you have taken a long vacation and are expected back any moment. I am sure I will continue to mark the days somehow. But all I know is that tonight I am alone. The pain is very real. And I miss my husband desperately.

We Are the Champions

It has been eleven months since you died.

Eleven months since my world stood still and I began to look at things differently.

Eleven months of counting the days since I last saw that big smile, heard that booming laugh. Eleven months since you winked at me, melting my heart and giving me a calm assurance that everything was going to be all right, only seconds before your last breath.

In 1957, the Auburn Tigers won a national championship. In 1958, you were born. You lived your entire life waiting to see them win another one. You were one of their fiercest fans. Obnoxious, to be quite honest. On January 10, 2011, eleven months after you died, the Auburn Tigers won their second national championship. As Ali said, "What a way to bookend your life."

Andrew and I have just returned from Auburn this afternoon where yesterday we were part of the championship celebration at Jordan Hare Stadium. Over 78,000 fans were there to watch the trophies come home to the Loveliest Village. We celebrated our heroes. We watched footage from the undefeated season. The Iron Bowl. SEC Game. The BCS championship game. Seeing the utter joy on the faces of the students who were allowed onto the field. The pride of the old players who returned to celebrate and honor the current coaches and players. The euphoria of the family united for one cause—*Auburn*—was overwhelming.

Being on the field with our press passes reminded me of the days when I was your camera assistant and we would travel down to Auburn to cover football for the TV station. I have such sweet memories of "working" with you. I loved watching you in action, doing your job. I remember the good times we had when Auburn won. But I also remember a couple of bad trips when the game did not end well. I remember going into the press conference and listening to you ask difficult questions, especially to Coach Tuberville, questions that I didn't want you to ask. You were doing your job, but I wanted you to give the man a break.

When we stepped into that press room yesterday, it was as if the torch had been passed from the father to the son. Although the room was familiar, the players were different. Gone was Tuberville and Housel. The old coach who always seemed to be offended by any question that was asked of him and the athletic director who tried to run him off under the cover of darkness. And there sat Gene Chizik and Jay Jacobs, the new coach that everyone is in love with for the moment and the AD that has suddenly gone from jeers to cheers. And Auburn is better for it.

Now the man behind the camera asking questions in the press room is our son. He has learned well from his father, and he is most defiantly his father's son. But he is coming into his own identity rather wonderfully. I loved my weekend with him. What a blessing it was to sneak away together. I realize these times are getting fewer and farther between.

In my mind, I can see you smiling.

February 20, 2011

Today was a mirror image of that Saturday fifty-two weeks ago. The last day we spent together outside of a hospital. The weather was perfect. I spent today by myself. Most of my thoughts going back to you and all that we did that last beautiful day.

We slept late and laid in the bed together. Ate breakfast at Gibson's with your mom. We went to Wal-Mart. You washed and vacuumed out your car. You spent a long time in the yard with Darby. Then you grilled steaks for supper, and we watched the Olympics. Then we went to bed early.

It was such a good day. A sweet time together. You felt so good . . . looked so much better than you had in weeks. Maybe months. You were so funny that day. We laughed more than we had in a long while.

It was the last memory I have of being totally happy with my life—our life together. Wasn't it so good and kind of God to provide that last beautiful day for us? Still missing you madly.

But healing has begun.

Tuesday, February 22, 2011

I go to bed tonight thankful for many things in my life.

Looking back one year ago, when I laid my head on these very pillows and covered them . . . soaked them with tears, thinking about what my future looked like without you. That night I could not imagine the following days, much less the coming year or anything past that to include my future.

But here I am. One year later. God in His mercy and faithfulness has proven to be everything His word promised that He would be to me. He has never left me or forsaken me. Even when I have felt alone here in my world and He has been silent, I have never felt abandoned by my Lord and Savior.

Every need I have had has been met in every shape, form, and fashion. I have not gone without. Our children are all well and thriving. We are healing, not whole or where we want to be yet, but healing is taking place.

There is joy and gladness in my heart. And I am no longer defined by grief and sadness. When I think of you, I remember our life together, I remember your laughter. My mind does not see you in the ICU. Of course, there are times I wish I could do over, but I do not have deep regrets or wish I had said more, loved you more, done more. I remember how happy we were, the way your laughter filled our home, your smile, and so many other wonderful things from our life together. Not a perfect life, but a life we were building and working hard as a team to make good. *"Good to great"* as they say.

As this day ends, I am thankful for so many things. Not just that this first year without you has ended. But I am thankful for this year, odd as that may sound. But in the past 365 days, I have learned more about the Lord than I ever have before and more about myself than I ever dreamed I would learn.

I am so guilty of making resolutions at the beginning of a new year, and within a few weeks they have been cast aside. On December 31, 2009, I wrote the following words: *In this coming year, I want to come to know my Savior. Because how can you truly trust someone who you have not fully developed a genuine relationship with? I grew up in the church. I have been afforded every advantage there is from a Christian standpoint. Yet I find myself so often taking my Christian heritage for granted. My most earnest hope is that in the process of developing a more genuine relationship with my Lord in this new year, I will be able to release these fears I am clinging to concerning you. Concerning our future. Concerning us. Concerning me.*

Inside one of the cards we received after your death, the following words were written: "Allow GOD to carry you through this, and on the other side of the pain there will be joy again."

We are finding Him to be a faithful Father.

There is joy again. And tonight, I am thankful.

The Road to Healing

Lately I've been reflecting on where God has taken me since you died. I am constantly amazed at His mercy and tender care for me on this road He has chosen for me to travel.

Although you are still the first thing on my mind when I wake in the morning, I no longer dread waking up for fear of facing the deep ache in my soul each day. Nor do I prolong sleep because of the impending torment of laying in the bed alone with the lights off and thinking of you . . . your body in the ground covered by dirt. I know you are not there in spirit. But the body of the man I so dearly love . . . that is where I left you. Odd, how the evil one knows just where to attack us when we are the most vulnerable.

As I said, God's tender love for me, most evident in the dark of night . . . has been such a constant during these days of healing. I know there are still many more days ahead on this road, but because of my past experiences with Him, I am confident He will meet me there.

On the road to healing.

Darby the Wonder Dog

Your sweet Darby has died. She was sick most of the summer but was able to rebound last week when we were all together for July 4th. All those years she was so afraid of loud noises and her own shadow. You would have loved watching her when we started the fireworks at the end of the family reunion. It was as if she was trying to jump up in the sky and catch the colored lights.

Truthfully, I expected this, months ago. She has mourned your death in such a profound way. Never truly getting back to her old self since the first night . . . but then none of us have.

Darby, the wonder dog . . . she was a wonderful dog.

~ 2012 ~

Two Years

A key component of faith is accepting without understanding.

Psalm 27:13–14, "I would have despaired unless I had believed that I would see the goodness of the LORD in the land of the living. Wait for the LORD; Be strong and let your heart take courage; Yes, wait for the LORD."

Two years today. We still miss you so much. And yet, God is still god. He is faithful. His word is true. We are blessed beyond measure.

No, our life is not the same. But yes, we have seen the goodness of the LORD! Joy has returned to our hearts. As the song says, "It is well with my soul."

Yes, it is well.

Fly Over

On the days when you were sent with a reporter to cover news from the sky, I usually got so nervous I would be nauseous. You were always in the air longer than you said you would be. And waiting for you to let me know you were safely back on the ground made me feel worse. All the different and terrible scenarios playing in my mind. But you loved every minute of it. You thrived on the rush and thrill.

I was working in Birmingham earlier today and as I was leaving my appointment a news chopper flew by. They were flying low enough that I could see the photographer leaning out the side with the camera on his shoulder. I thought of you. And I could hear you reassuring me after each flight that you were safe.

Even though your daredevil, throw caution to the wind attitude caused me to question your safety, I miss those days.

I just miss you.

In My Dreams

It was several months after you died before you appeared in my dreams. I was so physically, mentally, and emotionally exhausted after the memorial service that I don't remember if I even had any dreams during those first days and weeks. For many nights, sleeping was initially nonexistent. Almost mimicking your sleep pattern in the last weeks of your life.

The first time I dreamed of you we were at your mom's house. Everyone was at the table eating dinner. And as always, when you throw open the back door we all yelled, "Tom!"

I was so stunned to see you. I jumped up from the table and hugged you so tight. I couldn't believe you were there. I kept asking over and over "where have you been." That's when you grabbed my face in your hands and said, "Dana, don't you know? I've been with Jesus. I just came to tell you I'm okay. And I want you to know that you will be okay too. Dana, Jesus is real. Trust Him."

And then I woke up.

Three

Three years today, 365 multiplied by 3 is equal to 1095 days, and I have missed you every single one of them. So in memory of you, today I am going to "Play That Funky Music," drink a Diet Coke, eat sausage and pepperoni pizza, and watch *Jeopardy*. And then I will suffer through a two-hour documentary about some old battle I have never heard of on The History Channel.

Thanks for the lifetime of wonderful memories that you left for us.

Especially for those four little blessings called "The A Team." All my love.

Heal the Wound but Leave the Scar

When I look at my wrist, I cannot physically feel the pain that preceded the scar left by a hot iron. But I do remember how badly it hurt. When I look at my wrist and run my fingers over the scar, I don't just remember the sacrifice that was made so Amy could attend the out of state private Christian college; I also see the glow from sheer and unashamed pride that is all over her daddy's face. I remember the tears of joy streaming down my cheeks and leaving my dress wet as she walked across the outdoor stage on that beautiful spring morning. I look at the scar and am almost overcome with gratitude for all the ways God faithfully met the needs of our family during those four years. I look at my wrist and think that I never want to forget all that the scar represents.

Today Daddy and I attended the funeral of one of our business associates. My senses were heightened and my emotions close to overflowing because today is also exactly three and a half years since death entered our lives and took you to be with the Lord. As I observed the grieving family, even behind the laughter and smiles that sweet stories of remembrance provided, I could see the all too familiar pain on their faces and deep sadness in their eyes. And I thought about the long days ahead for each of them. Though the scars of death are not physically visible nor is the pain as gut-wrenching, they are both nonetheless a part of the lives of each member of our family. But today considering the faces of our adult children, I can see all the ways God has gently loved and provided for each of them . . . and their momma. Bringing each of us through the freshness of pain that was so intense it was almost paralyzing, to a place of remembering with peace and thanksgiving. And although the tears still come periodically for all of us, they are quickly wiped away with the gift of laughter.

Sitting in the church this afternoon, I realized that whether the wound is due to a broken heart from a failed relationship, consequences of our own poor life choices, health issues, death, or circumstances beyond our control, we all have scars that mark our lives—some visible and others unseen. If only we could grasp the idea that the key to healing, for all of us, is to stop picking at the scab that encourages infection in our individual lives. True healing can only come when we place our faith and trust, our hearts and lives, in the nailed scared hands of the One who died so that we might have life. And live it abundantly. May we all ask Him to heal our wounds but leave the scar so that we never forget His priceless gift of redemption and salvation.

> *Heal the wound but leave the scar*
> *A reminder of how merciful You are*
> *I am broken, torn apart*
> *Take the pieces of this heart*
> *And heal the wound but leave the scar* (Point
> of Grace)

The Plan: It Just Is What It Is

Earlier today I was reading a blog, and the writer said the following: *"I will be the first to admit, I spend most of my time surrounded by 'sameness.' Many of the people I am with day to day are very similar to me. I don't think that's necessarily bad or good—it's just what it is."*

At a time when I am feeling almost desperate for the Lord to do something new and wonderful in my life, I can so totally identify with the thoughts expressed above. We are a society that lives by a deadline. Reports must be submitted; appointments cannot be missed; pressure to perform our jobs better; produce more income so we can pay off our credit cards, mortgages, and student loans; and pad our savings for the future—all cause us to be held captive to our plans and self-imposed deadlines. We have become so accustomed to the demands of our own making that we often put a timetable on the Lord's working in our hearts and lives.

Within mere hours of your death, I began receiving books on dealing with grief. I was told the timeline of each stage of the mourning process. And I was given examples of people who did not allow enough time before making decisions about housing, careers, and what to do with everything that belonged to the deceased. And of course, the endless examples of those who did not allow the "proper time" to pass before they began dating and oh my goodness the nerve of them to go out and find love again! Clearly, prior to finding myself in this sorority of widows I could be found guilty of pointing my finger at others who broke the "advertised rules of grieving."

But truthfully, we've all been guilty of having expert thoughts and opinions about something we've never experienced. On any given Saturday between September and January, I am much smarter than 99 percent of the referees and umpires at college football games. And yet I've never played the sport, never officiated a single game. I scream and yell at the men in the black and white striped shirts who make split second decisions that affect the outcome as if I, sitting in my boatload of wisdom with my vast supply of knowledge, would make a different call if I were in the middle of the action.

Accordingly, I also found myself so very guilty of trying to put my expectations toward our children into play when you died. It took me many months to realize that they would not all grieve and process your death the same way. I fully expected that each one would move through grief in the same manner and according to the same time schedule. But that is not how it happened.

Although you were father to all four of them, you had a different relationship with each one of them. It took me a while to realize that even though they each loved you deeply and miss you in an excruciatingly painful way, because they are each a uniquely different and individual person, their processing of grief would therefore be uniquely different and individual. Sometimes as the author of the blog said *"it just is what it is,"* and we can't change it.

But here is what I have come to realize in the last forty-three months, it is good to have a plan of action. It is good to have goals, desires, and dreams. They are planted in our hearts by the Lord. But we must remember that God moves according to His plan and despite what my plan is . . . His plan is always better. Do I cringe when people, and sometimes people who I really don't know very well, ask, "So, are you seeing anybody? Have you found anyone yet? Do you think you will *ever* get married again?" Yes, I dread those conversations. Not because I am ashamed that no, I am not dating anyone. And yes, I do believe that one day I will marry again. But somehow, I always get the feeling that I have deviated from their plan for me. That I am not acting or living according to what they expect of me. And that I need to be fixed . . . quickly. Because we have a deadline to meet.

To be totally honest, I have been blessed to spend time with some very nice men. And I am thankful for each experience that I have had. But as the Facebook status for relationships says, it's complicated. Death complicates things. And sometimes in life "it just is what it is." Am I growing tired of the sameness in my life? Yes. I've not made a secret to the fact that my life no longer looks as I thought it would now. And quite honestly, I am weary of being instructed by God's word to "wait on the Lord." I am ready for something new and amazing. I am ready for my hopes and desires to come to fruition.

Despite the wonderful family and friends I have in my life, my heart is lonely. And to deny that it is so would be dishonest. But maybe in the waiting, the Lord is teaching me to be content in Him. Maybe He wants me to realize that what looks like "the sameness" each day is His tender mercies that are new each day. That the waiting is His protection on my life. And that His immeasurable love for me can fill every lonely space in my heart and life . . . if I will take my eyes off my plan and focus on Him.

> *"Because of the Lord's great love we are not consumed, for his compassion's never fail. They are new every morning; great is your faithfulness"* (Lamentations 3:22–23).

The Itsy-Bitsy Spider

The itsy-bitsy spider
Climbed up the water spout
Down came the rain
And washed the spider out
Out came the sun
And dried up all the rain
And the itsy-bitsy spider
Climbed up the spout again[18]

Grief never ends. I feel as if I am constantly forced to reset my mind and emotions. Processing and adjusting what has become my new normal is often exhausting.

There are so many days when I have felt like the spider, slowly climbing up the water spout. I work hard to reach the top, using muscles I never knew I had. Willing myself to take one more step. To hang on for one more day. As I make progress, without fail I begin to hear the rumbling of a storm in the distance. By the time I reach the top, the storm has been upgraded to a monsoon. Then suddenly any progress I've made is quickly forgotten, and I am caught in the flooding. When the clouds dissipate and the sun comes out, I find myself swept down the drain and lying on the sidewalk—sunburned and parched.

I am destroyed again.

Wash. Rinse. Repeat.

Grief never ends.

---

[18] The Itsy Bitsy Spider, Arthur Walbridge North 1910

Four Years

After you died, our family gathered around your hospital bed and we sang a song that I can't remember the name of or recall the words to now. Then we had a time of prayer, thanking God for the man He had allowed into our hearts and lives. I held your hand until it was cold, and I was told I could not stay with you any longer. I left your room, and in the hall of the CICU we began to put into motion the plans you and I discussed many months before that day.

Early the next morning, our four adult children were all in their beds at our house, sleeping . . . or attempting to sleep. The bag of hamburgers from Burger King that I had insisted on getting were sitting on the kitchen counter, untouched. Later that day, we would laugh that it seemed so appropriate that I would leave the hospital where you had just died and go buy hamburgers and french fries. The food that I had for so long begged you not to eat, suddenly became comfort food to me.

It had been what seemed like twelve years, but it had been only twelve hours since the landscape of our world forever changed. I was tossing and turning in our bed with April there clinging to me. She had flown home from Aspen earlier in the evening knowing that her daddy had died and having to grasp the reality of your death alone on a crowded plane.

Ali and Andrew had driven in from Nashville together but did not arrive in time. Amy was the one that the Lord intended to be with me that day. There with me when we were told nothing else could be done. There when we realized the end of your earthly life had come. This was how God planned it to be. And although I would have wanted each of them there with me, with their daddy, God's plan was best.

To their momma's heart, it seemed cruel that we had not all been together, but each of them was right where God had intended for them to be at that moment. So trying not to disturb April's much needed rest, I got up and went to the kitchen with my Bible and my computer to write. My therapy for so many months.

As I have spent the last few weeks reading over my words, during that time I continue to be amazed at the goodness of the Lord. Even in the difficulty we lived through during your dialysis and then death, God was so merciful to our family. Sending exactly who we needed to be an encouragement to us. Nudging so many of our family and friends to open their hearts to share wonderful, funny, and most often goofy stories of the man we love so much. Providing moments of laughter and silliness amidst the pain and gut-wrenching grief. Drawing our children and I into a tighter bond with our family than we had ever experienced. And showing us the unconditional love of dear friends who were hurting as well.

Although these four years without you have been the most difficult and painful times we have ever experienced, your children and I are doing well. Our lives, though different from what we had each planned, are quite happy and contented. Our sovereign Lord has been faithful to each of us individually and as a family. And we are thankful for His mercies that are new every day. We are blessed. Jesus. Never. Fails.

I'll Be Okay

Death has a way of allowing you to blot out some things that you would rather not confront, giving you an excuse to romanticize what was. I must confess that it's easy to only write about the good times you and I shared, recounting only the carefully selected funny stories. To only talk of the sweet, tender photos depicting a relationship that appears to be without conflict.

Appears to be . . .

We married very young, and we did a lot of growing up together as husband and wife. But in many ways, we were both still immature children, each of us possessing a healthy dose of selfishness and pride. Wanting our own way and at times willing to momentarily sacrifice one another's happiness to see our individual desires succeed.

But I can honestly say that over the course of our almost thirty-year marriage, those times were outnumbered 2–1 by the days we were loving and respectful . . . supportive and giving of ourselves, rather than taking what we wanted and tearing each other down in the process.

Life's difficulties and pains can be used to strengthen your relationship or divide you into warring tribes. We certainly had our share of those days. Times when lines were drawn in the sand with a harsh word or most often my very loud and expressive (and not so very mature) body language.

But along the way, we also learned about forgiveness and grace. Bending but not to the point of breaking. Accepting each other's flaws as easily as we embraced each other's strengths. I do not embellish our story when I say it was very good and I am blessed to have been yours. I am thankful for the life I had as your wife and friend. Each day spent with you was ordained by God to prepare me to spend the second half of my life without you. I believe I've been prepared well.

Yes, I really do believe I'll be okay.

All Things New

He who was seated on the throne said, "I am making
everything new!" Then he said, "Write this down,
for these words are trustworthy and true."
—Revelation 21:5

In His time, He is honoring His promise. I am writing it down
so everyone will know of His faithfulness. Beauty from ashes. All
things new.

Flashback. Saturday June 21, 1980.
I have no memory of sleeping the night before. At six thirty that
morning, with my wedding dress and suitcase packed to bursting
open in the trunk, I left my parents' home and drove to the church.

Those involved with our day hated us for the early wake up
call. But on that very hot June morning, we got married before most
people had been awake long enough to enjoy their second cup of
coffee! *It was a new dawn. It was a new day. It was a new life . . . for
us. And we were feeling good.*

> *See, I am doing a new thing! Now it springs
> up; do you not perceive it?*
> *I am making a way in the wilderness and
> streams in the wasteland. (Isaiah 43:19)*

Fast-forward thirty-four years. Saturday, June 21, 2014

"It's a new dawn . . ." I am quite wordy and seldom do I find it difficult to express a thought or emotion. But today "thankful, blessed, and honored" seems so trite and grossly inadequate. The spiritual covering and unconditional acceptance my parents have provided me during the days of grief, sorrow, rest, and healing is a treasure beyond any kind of measure or comparison. I am astounded by their selfless love for me. I have had the special joy of peering through a secret window into their lives. I have been witness to the sweetness of their day to day devotion to each other, as well as their faithfulness to the Lord. As a young child in their home, I did not recognize their examples of selfless love for what they were. As their adult child, these moments have become a beautiful and priceless gift.

"It's a new day . . ." Thinking back on the life I shared with you and the sweet blessings that our relationship produced, I have so much to be thankful for. When I chose to leave our home and move in with my parents, I had no idea how the last three years would help me to find that peaceful balance of respect for what brought me to this place . . . and an incredible hope and excitement for the *new blessings* that lie ahead.

"It's a new life, for me . . ." I find myself once again making lists and checking them twice. For a couple of weeks, I have been packing my suitcase and what will probably end up being 500 boxes and preparing to leave my parents' home. I am physically and figuratively heading to a *new place*. I have accepted a job offer in a city a few miles from home. I can tell you that I am covered in peace and assurance that my steps are being guided by the Lord. And I am excited about the possibilities this position will provide me.

This is an opportunity to do what I have longed for—something *new*, something creative. Something totally unexpected.

"And I'm feeling good . . ." In just a few weeks, I will pull out of the driveway and point my car toward Houston, Texas—a new city that I will call home. I don't think I've slept longer than forty-five minutes since I went to bed last night. The words from the song

"Feeling Good[19]" are stuck on repeat in my head. The lyrics perfectly express what I am feeling at three thirty on a Saturday morning in a hotel in Houston as I confidently prepare to step out in faith toward my *new adventure.*

My heart is filled with *a new joy* because of this *new thing* that God ordained just for me when He laid the foundation of the earth. This morning, on our thirty-fourth anniversary, I am looking back with a heart of thanksgiving for the life we shared—for the joys and trials, triumphs and defeats we lived through together because they prepared me well for this new chapter in my life.

---

[19] Nina Simone, Feeling Good 1965

Thanksgiving 2014

This season of the year, it's easy for each of us to acknowledge the blessings we have been afforded in our lives. It's natural for us to express our thanksgiving when all around us we are reminded of the day we are celebrating. However, it is much more difficult to remember those blessings when times are tough. When hardship is all we see. When sadness, pain, grief, confusion, and uncertainty are the emotions and experiences we are walking through. Often, it is easier to see the goodness and blessings only when life is grand and free of struggle and difficulty.

On January 1st, I started my jar of blessings. I wanted to be able to look back over 2014 and see how often I realized God's favor over me during the new year. At first it was the big and happy days that I was thankful for. The days when our children would call with fabulous news about their careers or new friends that had been placed in their lives. It was a praise for good health reports from those who had been experiencing challenges, physically or emotionally. It is easy to celebrate a new job, new city, and renewed hopes. But often it was little things—things that I would have disregarded if I had not been conscious to look for blessings every day. What I have learned is that it is all too easy to label our day or our lives as *#blessed* or *#happy* when life is good and easy. But it is in the long days of *#sadness, #hopeless, #discouraged, #lonely* that if we look closely enough we see the faithfulness of someone who never leaves us or forsakes us, regardless of what hashtag we use to describe our existence.

Today, I am thankful for the blessings of our children who are happy and content in their careers, for the opportunities and the adventures that they are experiencing in their individual lives. I am thankful for my parents who have invested in my life and loved each other unconditionally for fifty-seven years, for the example they have set for me of a life of excellence and honor.

I am thankful for my extended family who loves and supports me in prayer and verbal encouragement. For lifelong friends who have stood by me in days of sadness and days of celebration. For new friends that have brought a breath of fresh air into my life. For new experiences in a new place that gives me renewed hope and bigger dreams than I have ever had. For all of this and so much more . . . I am thankful. I am blessed.

Just as King David proclaimed in the Old Testament, "He has put a new song in my mouth, a song of praise to our God," may we each proclaim His goodness and everlasting mercy in and on our lives.

Even on the days when we don't see it or feel it.

Five

Slowly five minutes became five hours . . . then five days, weeks, and months. Even though we thought we would never make it five minutes, we have arrived at five years. Not just surviving, but each of us thriving and healing. Not just existing but living, laughing, embracing, and finding joy in God's oftentimes puzzling yet perfect plan for our lives.

Five years.

We miss you. We always will. But as April recently wrote on her blog, "We hold on to hope. We hold on to a peace that passes all understanding. We hold on to the faithfulness of our heavenly Father."

Jeremiah 31:13, "I will turn their mourning into gladness; I will give them comfort and joy instead of sorrow."

Yes, He has.

Father's Day and our Anniversary

"Dads are like chocolate chip cookies. They may have chips or be totally nutty, but they are sweet and make the world a better place. Especially for their children"

On what would have been our thirty-fifth wedding anniversary, we also celebrate Father's Day. Today I'm remembering the sweet and totally nutty father of my children. A man with enough confidence in who you were that you were never afraid for us to see the chips in your armor. I am thankful for the life we shared and the legacy you left for our children. Our world is better because you were in it.

You loved us well. We miss you still.

We will love you forever.

Be Still

Earlier this evening I was talking to someone about how I've spent this past year here in Houston. I said that these days have been so good for me in several ways. But mostly because I could just sit and be quiet. To *be still*.

My life has been spent in relationships. I was your wife for thirty years. I've been a mom for thirty-four years. Both of these roles were and continue to be my dream job and the place where I am the most fulfilled. I was blessed with the opportunity to nurture, to love, encourage, cheer for, fight for, and support the ones dearest to me. But as I have learned too well, in the blink of an eye life changes. I am no longer a wife. My babies are all in their thirties and no longer require so much from me. It feels like my role now is to *be still*.

I've been clueless about how to even do that. What did it mean? *Be still.* Does it equate to being lazy and uninvolved in life around me? After our conversation, I looked back through my private journal and counted all the times I had noted a verse of scripture containing those words.

> The Lord will fight for you; you need only to be still. (Exodus 14:14)

> Be still . . . do not grieve. (Nehemiah 8:11)

> Meditate in your heart and be still. (Psalm 4:4)

Be still before the Lord and wait patiently for Him. (Psalm 37:7)

Be still, and know that I am God. (Psalm 46:10)

Be still, O inhabitants of the coast. (Isaiah 23:2)

Rest and be still. (Jeremiah 47:6)

Be still before the Lord, all mankind. (Zechariah 2:13)

Quiet! Be still! Then the wind died down and it was calm. (Mark 4:39)

Each of these verses appear in my journal over and over. Some of the references also included the following comments by me:

- Be still. Again. Really?
- Be still. I'm so tired of being still.
- Be still . . . what is God waiting on? What is He doing?
- I am so stinking tired of being told to be still!
- Are you kidding me, God? Be still. AGAIN?

I wish I could tell you that after more than 365 days of being instructed to *be still*, a great revelation has come to me and my life path and plans are now crystal clear and are more than I dared to dream. That I have my future precisely mapped out and every nook and cranny of my life makes so much sense. But that would be way too easy and it would also be a total lie. However . . .

Yes, I do have more clarity and direction. My spirit feels rested. And although there are still so many unknowns in my life, I'm no longer begging for action or answers. So maybe Exodus 14:14, "The Lord will fight for you; you need only to be still," is finally sinking in and taking hold of my heart and mind. The light bulb is on. I don't have to fight the fight alone. He will fight for me.

So this is me tonight—believing that whatever comes into my life will be worth being still for.

Roots and Wings

When our children were little, I often heard that I needed to give them roots and wings. "Roots to know where home is and wings to fly away, exercising what they have been taught." At the time, I thought giving them roots was the hard part. That once their wings had developed and they could navigate life independent of me, letting go would be easy.

It turns out I was very wrong.

As our children grew up and left home, I fooled myself into believing that I had mastered the "wings" part of the job. But the truth is, giving your child wings is really, really hard. Yes, there are great rewards and wonderful advantages to having adult children. But there is no way to sugarcoat or dress it up and make it look better . . . the hardest part of parenting is letting go. Giving them freedom to make their own decisions and then accepting those decisions is not always an easy path to travel. Our choices are no longer their choices. They will likely develop their own goals and embrace ideas and lifestyles different from what we would choose if we were still in the driver's seat of their lives.

We raised them to think independently and make choices based on their convictions. So why are we stunned when they do this? Or was our granting them freedom to live their lives something that was conditional? Were we only giving them freedom if they choose our goals, dreams, and ideas for their lives?

I'm reminded of the birds that made a nest on my parents' front porch a few years ago. Perched up high where the cross beams meet the corner posts, we watched a tiny family learn to live together in a mayonnaise jar. The momma bird so carefully tended her little ones, keeping them warm and bringing them food, protecting them from anyone and anything that would harm them. Over time, the little birds became curious about life outside the nest, and their baby heads began to poke out the top of the jar. We laughed when the ever-attentive mommy would swoop back in from her spot in a tree nearby and force their heads back down where it was safe. Until finally the day came when it was time to spread their wings. That same overprotective momma pushed her babies out of that environment of safety. And there from the top ledge of the front porch, she watched as those tiny wings began flapping with all their might and carried her little ones out into the wide-open spaces of the world—each one flying at a different height and speed, headed in different directions, chasing different dreams.

Learning to accept and love the differences between each of our children and myself is an ongoing process for me. Honestly, it's become an excruciating process. You see, three months ago, a rock was thrown through the window of our glass house. One of our little birds has flapped its wings of independence and has flown away from our family nest without looking back. Choosing to make a life that no longer includes me or 99.9 percent of our extended family and friends. The reasons for this disconnect are many and need to be held private. We are simply living in that place where "it just is what it is." Although I don't like it, I am learning to be okay with it. Giving our child the freedom that is needed right now.

Over the last few weeks as I have thought about the momma bird, I've wondered if she ever questions her actions. Does she regret teaching her little bird how to spread its wings and fly? Does she sit in her tree and wonder if she pushed too soon or too hard? Even though she may not know where the little bird is or what events are taking place in its life, does she have an inner peace in knowing she provided deep roots so that her little one could always find its way home?

I initially didn't want to talk about it or let anyone beyond our immediate family know what was going on. I was devastated and hurt. I was embarrassed and felt as if I had not done all I could to hold your family together in your absence. I felt a sense of shame, and I was angry. But as each day slowly passed, I realized that we are all broken. Every one of us. Every family has something that they deal with, something they hesitate to openly discuss. When I began to read about and listen to the stories of other families in turmoil, I realized that by being honest and transparent when sharing their lives, I was encouraged. I no longer felt ashamed. The more open I became with our struggle, the more I felt the anger and hurt began to fade away. By being honest and transparent about my pain and disappointment, I was able to release her to the Lord, trusting that He loves her so much more than we do and as His chosen child, He will never take His eyes off of her. And if it is His will that we will one day be in her life again, He will orchestrate reconciliation and restoration for each of us, in His perfect time.

Currently there is no communication between us. But I am at peace with her decision. I am clinging to the words from a song we grew up singing in church, "*His eye is on the sparrow, and I know He watches me.*"

Today I am thankful that His eyes is on our daughter . . . wherever she is. And I continue to pray that until He guides her safely home, He will wrap her in the warm blanket of His amazing love and protection that never fails.

I came to Psalm 145 in my reading this morning and was transported to another time . . .

On a cold and rainy Sunday in November 2009, we attended a seminar at St. Vincent's Hospital in Birmingham. It was a requirement for those seeking to be placed on the national kidney transplant waiting list. The last session of the day was on putting together an end of life plan. Along with all the other information we were processing that day, our group was told that once you make it past qualifying for transplant, the typical wait could be anywhere from five to seven years. And that in many cases the patient's health deteriorates and death occurs before a match can be found.

For much of our ride home that evening, except for my not so quiet sobbing, we sat in stunned silence. I'm not sure what either of us had expected before the meeting. However, I'm quite sure I never expected to leave there so discouraged. About thirty minutes after we left the hospital, you grabbed the pen that was tucked in the button placket of your light blue oxford cloth dress shirt, handed it to me and said, "Baby, I want you to be ready when it's time. We need to make the plan."

And so, on that dreary Sunday, headed north on I-65 we put everything in writing. With clarity and in detail, you told me what you wanted me to do if your life on earth did in fact come to an end. You planned every minute of the funeral service. You told me where you wanted to be buried. Things that would need to be done and who you wanted to do them. I clearly remember commenting that for someone who was not typically so detail-oriented you didn't leave out one detail in this fly-by-the-seat-of-your-pants plan you were throwing together. You stared at me for a minute then squeezed my hand. It was when you turned your head back toward the road that I noticed the tears that were threatening to spill down your right cheek. I realized then that your thoughts hadn't been thrown together at all. You had been formulating your end of life plan for some time.

For the memorial service, you said you wanted someone to read Psalm 145. Then quickly changed your mind and said, "No, erase that, sing the song." Three months later, on the last Thursday in February, our friend David led the music at the funeral. And just as requested, he sang the song so beautifully arranged by Travis Cottrell, "Forevermore" (Psalm 145).

The words of your favorite psalm were true when King David penned them. They were true when put to music. They are true today. They will be true tomorrow and forevermore. Isaiah 40:8 says, "The grass withers, the flower fades. But the word of our God stands forever."

If you were to ask me what is the greatest lesson I've learned since that rainy Sunday afternoon headed North on I-65, I would say it's that I now know with greater assurance that God's word is truth. In times of joy and sadness, darkness and light, His word never changes. He can be trusted. He is faithful . . . still.

You remain in our memories and in our hearts. Forevermore.

Six

February 22, 2016

Ali has been in town for the last few days, and we spent the weekend in Waco. Earlier today as we were traveling back to Houston, we discussed how the passage of time has a way of tricking your memory into thinking that some events happened only moments ago. While at the same moment also convincing you that those events occurred even farther in the past than they did.

Six years.

My heart remembers like it happened today. Yet it also seems so much further in the past that my mind can't recall things I never imagined I would forget. Life eventually becomes about the one you are in and no longer about the one you can never go back to. That in-between place of fresh, raw, and painful memories and the fog of the distant past. The farther away we get from the events that took place on this day six years ago, the more comfortable I become with the place and time God has chosen for me. But embracing the present while honoring the past and yet hoping for the future—like juggling knives—has not been easy or natural.

Yet regardless of my yesterday, today, or tomorrow, one constant remains . . . Jesus never changes.

And that simple truth is where peace and contentment are birthed.

The Long Road

I was five years old when we met in 1966. It's difficult for me to find even one part of the last fifty years that has not been affected by your presence and your death. Even now, over six years after you died, the memories haunt me. The tears come at unexpected and inconvenient times. I continue to believe that grief cannot be avoided. Unlike a traffic jam on the interstate, navigating through this process is not like using the GPS in my car. There are no alternate routes. Whatever is on the long and difficult road up ahead of me, I have no choice but to live it . . . every day.

Wish

On this warm September day, if a genie in a bottle gave me three wishes I would ask for: 1)the sound of your laughter, 2) the whisper of something silly in my ear during a serious moment, 3) a kiss on my neck.

I miss you.

Everyday

There's a cool crispness in the fall air. I wish you were here enjoying your favorite time of year.

My heart misses you.

Everyday.

"When you remember me, it means you have carried something of who I am with you, that I have left some mark of who I am on who you are. It means that you can summon me back to your mind even though countless years and miles stand between us. It means that if we meet again, you will know me. It means that even after I die, you can still see my face and hear my voice and speak to me in your heart" (Frederick Buchner).

Hopes and Dreams

For me, your death was not only an earthly physical death. But also, the death of our hopes, our dreams, and our plans. However, I am learning that God's hopes, dreams, and plans for me are bigger and greater than mine could ever be. But finding a way to turn pain and death into hopes and dreams again has not been easy. Even though you battled kidney disease all of our marriage, I never imagined there would be a time in my life that I wasn't married to you.

In the months and years since you died, I've made many mistakes along the way. In reconciling my singleness with my longing to be married again, I've grown impatient. Recognizing that my best yesterday belonged to you and my best today and tomorrow could possibly be with someone else, I've allowed my heart to go places it had no business going. Sometimes, hurting and lonely people make choices that they never set out to make.

Running ahead of God's will and opening my heart to a relationship that, buried deep beneath my loneliness, I knew did not honor the Lord set me up for a long and painful recovery. I am guilty of inserting my will and my desires into the equation. I tried to manipulate what I wanted into something that resembled what I thought was God's plan. No one else is to blame for my choices or my pain. Each came as a result of decisions that were mine alone. But even in this, God has used my disobedience to prove once again that He is a faithful, loving, and forgiving Father. And although He has not removed the desire to marry again, He has brought me to a place of contentment and peace as He is teaching me to be still and wait for His plan.

Being still and waiting are not easy for me. I often try to make my desires line up with what I want God's best to look like. Yet God continues to pierce my heart with these specific instructions. Be still. Wait.

My only choice is to obey His prompting and believe His very best will be far beyond my wildest hopes and craziest dreams.

I am trusting that His best plan for me will be worth the wait.

Seven

On Monday, February 22, 2010, when my life was changed forever, the following words were on our kitchen calendar: *"God may be invisible, but He's in touch. You may not be able to see Him, but He's in control. And that includes you, your circumstances. That includes what you've just lost. That includes what you've just gained. That includes all of life . . . past, present, future."*

Jeremiah 29:11, "For I know the plans I have for you declares the LORD, plans to prosper you and not to harm you, plans to give you a hope and a future."

What I have learned in the seven years since that day is this . . . His plans for me are perfect, even when I don't understand them. His word will light my path, even though I can't see Him. He will never fail me, even when I fail Him. He is always faithful. He can be trusted. He is my hope.

I miss you still.

I love you always.

Permanent

I started a new Bible study recently, and the following words jumped off the page at the exact moment I needed to read them:

> When you're in that place—clinging to the side of a wall made of rock, a storm of uncontrollable circumstances swirling around you—what you're holding on to becomes clear. Place your foot on shale, and it will crumble beneath you. Grab hold of a loose ledge, and your hand will slip. But hold tight to the mountain itself, and it will hold you up.
>
> God's promises are permanent when the worlds promises pass away. Gods covenant is permanent when our good intentions pass away. God's love is permanent when our good behavior passes away. God's mercy is permanent when our bodies pass away. God's hope is permanent when our plans are passing away. Gods sovereignty is permanent when our power is passing away. The gospel is permanent when our belief is passing away.
>
> Whatever this temporary life has looked like and whatever signs are waiting on the road ahead, God and His Truth will always be true. You cannot change truth. You cannot earn it or

lose it or escape it. But you can hold on to it, knowing that it holds you.[20]

Psalm 34:18 tells me, "He is near to the broken hearted." In the day of sadness and darkness, in the days of doubt and fear, in the days of sorrow and confusion, His tender nearness has been a blessing and comfort. He has brought me beauty for ashes, strength for fear, gladness for mourning, and peace for despair.

On Christ the solid rock I stand . . . all other ground is sinking sand.

---

[20] Passages from *She Reads Truth: Holding Tight to Permanent in a World That's Passing Away* by Raechel Myers and Amanda Bible Williams (Nashville TN: B&H Publishing Group, 2016).

Spring Gala 2017

Three days ago, with a special message from her daddy engraved on a charm hanging from a bouquet of flowers . . . our baby girl got married. I stood beside her as she pledged her love and her life to a very good man. The man you and I have prayed would come into her life, if the Lord so ordained. God has honored thirty-three years of prayers. Our new son-in-law is everything we had hoped and prayed for.

The service was very small and intimate. No more than a handful of people were there, just as the bride and groom had wanted. On Saturday night, they hosted a wedding dinner in their new backyard. The groom smoked brisket and pork. You would have been so proud of him; the meat was incredible. There were enough side dishes to feed an army, each one amazing. As it is often said when we are all together, it was said again that "Daddy would have loved this!"

It was such a lovely weekend peppered with brimming emotions because of the obvious hole in our hearts and lives. But once again, God faithfully provided a soothing balm that allowed us to joyfully celebrate covenant marriage and the blending of hearts and lives.

Thirty-Seventh Anniversary

There are times when I feel the need to go back and read through words I've previously written. Like a gauge, revisiting my thoughts is a way to prove to myself that I'm progressing. A confirmation that healing truly is taking place in my heart and life.

I recently came across something that I wrote six years ago, on our thirty-first anniversary. Rereading my words from that day no longer brings me sadness or heaviness of heart. But rather, a spirit of thankfulness for God's faithful and tender care for me in the long days, weeks, and years since I first began recording my thoughts.

June 20, 2011

During our life together I stood at the window hundreds of times and watched as you were riding the mower in the yard. Your head bobbing to the beat of whatever song you were singing. The golf towel you bought on our honeymoon at Sea Island was thrown across your shoulder. An Auburn cap on your head with a paper towel folded lengthwise and stuck inside to keep the sweat off your brow and out of your eyes. An old Steak Out cup filled with ice water sat in the cup holder. On the back of the mower, there was a pair of pruning shears that you would use to cut tree limbs or branches that had begun to grow into your path. You took great care to make sure you cut in just the right place. Often it made no sense to me that you would do this to a tree or bush. From my perspective, there appeared to be no growth in your way. So of course, I always questioned what you were doing because often it seemed as if you were just butchering a beautiful tree. With a touch of irritation, you would again explain that for it to grow fuller and more beautiful the limb *had to be pruned* because this was the only way new growth could take place.

God has been doing some pruning in my heart and life, and it's painful being in His garden.

David Jeremiah wrote the following: *"God allows no pain without purpose. Instead, He uses pain to dispense power. His power can rest upon you only when you've abandoned the idea that you're big enough to go it alone. You're not big enough; you'll never make it without depending utterly upon Him and going in His strength. You're destined to fail without righteousness and holiness. And some pruning must take place, with sharpened shears, to cut away those things that would prevent righteousness and holiness in your life. But how liberated you will be, how free to grow toward the heavens, after that pruning is accomplished!"*[21]

I remember Mr. Kilgo teaching us in seventh grade science that plants grow the most not during the beautiful and sunny days of spring and summer, or even in the slow gentle rains. They grow the most when the winds are fierce and the storms are raging. He said you could take a cross-section of the earth during a vicious storm and literally observe the roots reaching further down into the soil—digging in and holding on for dear life.

So I guess the question that's being asked of me is, *how far down do your roots go?* The storms of life are raging; the fierce winds are blowing all around you. Can you feel His love as He prunes back what would prevent you from growing more like Him? Are you trying to make it on your own strength? Or are you utterly dependent on Him? Digging in and holding on to Him for dear life is *the safest place you can be* when the storms appear.

God never wastes pain.

Andrew's twenty-sixth birthday was last week. Father's Day was yesterday, and tomorrow is our thirty-first anniversary. Each celebration without you represents yet another limb God has taken His shears to. Like a scab being ripped off a wound, exposing tender

---

[21] David Jeremiah, *When Your World Falls Apart*, W Publishing Group

flesh. Another opportunity for new growth to take place, allowing beauty to slowly return to our lives. Your children and I miss you so much. For each of us, the pruning seems cruel and so very harsh. New growth is slow and not only is it uncomfortable, it often hurts to the point of being unbearable. But even during our pain, we are sustained by God's word that promises his love for us is deeper than we can understand.

His love is beyond measure.

June 21, 2017 . . . at the park down the street from where I live, there's a huge tree with beautiful lush green leaves on it. Once you get close to it, you can see there are places all over the trunk where people have carved their initials. The bark has grown around all the letters, and the exposed wood has weathered over time. Yet this tree has grown tall and strong despite the scars caused by the sharp instrument. Today, on what would have been our thirty-seventh anniversary, I can see and feel the scars that grief has produced in my heart and life. As expected, there are still times when it's painful to remember what was, and trying to move past what will never be is often very difficult. But through His tender care during the fiercest of storms, God has allowed growth to take place.

Since moving to Houston, I've discovered that storms in the Gulf of Mexico often produce a nice cool evening breeze that makes a lovely sound as it blows through the leaves on the palm trees near my house. Today, a sweet song of contentment and peace is blowing through the new leaves that have recently begun to bloom on the scared tree of my life.

And . . . *it is well with my soul.*

July 2017

Another July 6 has arrived and I am once again awake very early at my parents' house. As I pack for my flight back to Houston later today, there is only excitement as I think about going back to my life in Texas. Remembering the two things that caused me the most fear on the day I moved out of my comfort zone . . . the fear that I would spend the rest of my life alone and the fear that I would not make it financially . . . those are still concerns.

Three years later I am still alone, but not lonely. God has provided new relationships that I would never have experienced had I not moved here. My world has grown and been enriched by each blessing of friendship that I have made. Financially, God has never failed to supply what I need when I need it. Never providing excess before the need, but never meeting the need too late. He has proven time and time again that He can be trusted. He is faithful. Whether the provision is of a job and boss that I love or dear friends to meet a desperate need for companionship.

He has been faithful.

Death Changes the Living

It doesn't happen often. I can count on one hand the number of times in the last seven years that you have appeared in my dreams. And suddenly this week you've shown up two nights in a row.

Waking up happens too soon and feels like saying goodbye all over again. The pain is no longer as deep but still it's there, lingering on the fringes of my thoughts all day. Hours later, my emotions remain on the brink of overflowing, like floodgates threatening to break open.

Your death has become as much of who I am . . . who I'm becoming, as your life was. There is nothing easy, neat, or simple about it. Grieving you has been hard, messy, and complicated. Sprinkled throughout the day to day new normal of life without you, there are still days that can only be explained as difficult. The path between sorrow and joy is a lifelong journey filled with potholes and smooth surfaces. Reminding me of what was and what will never be.

Death changes the living. There will never be a day when I don't think of you, miss you, and love you deeply. But the day has come when the sadness caused by your presence in my dreams and the pain produced by your physical absence from my life no longer paralyze or define me.

I miss you desperately. But I am also happy. My life and heart are filled with joy, laughter, and love. Understanding or explaining how so many deep emotions can coexist is a difficult task. But each emotion has become guilt-free—each reminding me that our life together was very good. A confirmation that even in your absence my life can still be very good.

Grieving your death has brought a brokenness that's produced healing and hope, which only comes from the Lord. So many days it felt as if I was falling backward in slow motion. But Jesus has shown up each day. He has been my comfort and my guide. My faithful friend in moments too heartbreaking for words. Providing strength, rest, and guidance when I have been weak, weary, and wandering without direction.

Psalm 34:18, "The Lord is close to the broken-hearted and saves those who are crushed in spirit."

Giving Thanks

From our first Thanksgiving in 1978 when I was a senior in high school, through the last one you celebrated with us in 2009, we spent thirty-one Thanksgiving Days together. I look at photos from that autumn day, and I do not see a man who was just three short months from the end of his earthly life. I see a man with a servant heart who loved his family well. A man who was joyful in the midst of great pain and physical difficulty. A man who taught us how to laugh through our tears. I see you. The you who remained constant, steady, and resolved until you laughed one last time and drew your final breath. I see my man, my children's daddy. A man who lived his life in such a way that even in the depths of our grief the life you lived continues to remind us we have so many reasons to be thankful during this season, and every day we are blessed to live.

"Give thanks to the LORD, for He is good; His love endures forever" (1 Chronicles 16:34),

The Final Letter

Dear Tom,

I loved who I was as your wife. I loved the intimacy of our thirty years of marriage, the physical and emotional. I loved that we could be at an event, on separate sides of the room and making eye contact, you would wink at me. And how we could read each other's expressions. I loved the feeling of belonging to you. I loved that you were mine. And I loved the sense of security you provided for me. The feel of your hand on the curve of my back leading me by gently pushing me ahead. I loved us and I loved who I was because of you.

Grieving your death has softened me in many ways, and yet also toughened me at the same time. I've been forced to stand on my own two feet and make the decisions that I had so willingly deferred to you as the head of our home, to make for us. Moving away from the umbrella of safety and protection that I have always experienced has stretched me personally and spiritually. I thought I was moving to Houston so that our children would see me as more than a wife and mom. I desperately wanted to make them proud of me. I realize now that I needed this life change to prove to myself that I have gifts and talents beyond my comfort zone. And even though I still have no clue how to program the TV with the remote control or how to grill a steak, our children were proud of me long before I changed zip codes.

Although the calendar tells me it's been eight years since you died, in many ways it seems like less. I guess that's because during those first four years, I was loved, protected, and cared for so well. I wasn't grieving alone because so many people were there with me, and we all grieved together. Yet regardless of how wonderful that covering was, at times it was almost smothering. It's embarrassing that I would even hint of being too loved. I do realize the blessing I've been given to have so many in my life who care very deeply for me. So many who have honored you by standing in the gap your absence has left. It's just that so often I've felt like there's been a neon sign with the word WIDOW flashing over my head, or I've felt lost and alone in the crowd. Moving to Houston was a way for me to discover who I am without you, to build my new unplanned life without our children and our family by my side. Like a butterfly breaking out of the chrysalis that for a period had been its protective shell.

As I've said before, when I left Alabama I felt like a recent high school graduate moving away for the first time. I've been forced to take care of myself and make adult decisions that I never had to make before. For so long I have maintained that Houston was not going to be my forever place but rather the place where I would spread my butterfly wings and figure out who I am as this person on her own. But if my time in Texas is my time away at college, then like many college students when discouragement and lone-liness have come, I too have tried to drop out and move home. But each time, my heavenly Father has intervened and the door to leave has never opened enough for me to walk through it.

In each moment of discouragement and doubt, God has faithfully provided for me. I never could have imagined that I, a confirmed stay-at-home wife and mom with no desire for a career, could be so happy and content with a 9–5 job. The Lord has placed me in an amazing work situation where I feel valued and appreci-ated. I am part of a team where opportunities for growth and greater responsibility for others on our team are being entrusted with me. Daily, I feel that I am gaining confidence in my ability to perform my job, and I have been blessed with a boss who, not only loves Jesus and respects me, also validates my efforts and contributions to his business, making it known that he feels blessed the Lord lead me to his team.

But isn't it just like God to bring us, kicking and screaming like a toddler, to a place we never wanted or dreamed we would be and through His tender and patient leading we find unex-pected contentment? Slowly over the last two years I have begun to see that if it's God's plan, Houston could easily be my forever place. And while that thought no longer causes me to be fearful but rather hopeful and eager, it also does not come without mixed emotions. Because it now seems that God is once again stirring within my heart a new desire. As if He is leading me in a different direction . . . all over again. I'm at that familiar crossroads facing many of the unknowns that have frequently kept me awake in the dark of night. I find myself asking questions that still produce no reasonable answers. At least answers that can be seen with my earthly eyes and processed by my finite mind.

In the middle of all the mounting unknowns and seeming uncertainty about my future, deep in my heart there is also a touch of excitement and a lingering sense of peace. I believe He has purposed with a good and gracious design, every joyful and painful event in my life. It is because of this deep assurance in His sovereignty that I am excited to see where His dreams and plans for me will lead. I have no idea what my life will look like in the coming days, weeks, and years. But because looking back at His faithfulness brings me peace, there is peace in knowing He will continue to be faithful. Peace in knowing firsthand that even in the painful and difficult times, His character is only ever good and gracious. There is peace in knowing that He will provide for me and that I can trust Him with my life. There is peace.

I was listening to the song "He Leadeth Me" in my car recently . . .

My heart attests your loveliness
In summer sun or winters gloom
In darkest times where I can't see
Still by God's hand, He leadeth me
He leadeth me! He leadeth me!
By His own hand He leadeth me;
His faithful follower I would be,
For by His hand He leadeth me

I thought about the subtitle I have given to this collection of letters, *God's Faithfulness in Every*

Season of Grief. I can clearly see His hand leading me through every day and every season since you died. In the frozen, dark gloom of winter. In the spring when everything is fresh and new. In the hot drought of summer when life is dry and parched. In the beauty and the cool crispness of fall, by His hand He has been leading me.

There's one other line in the song that resonates with me, "In death's cold wave I will not flee / Still by God's hand, He's leading me!" It's so very true. Even in the cold river of sadness and the suffocating weight of loss, when I was stumbling through the thick fog of grief, He has never let go of my hand.

My sweet, goofy man, although I loved who I was with you and never wanted that to change . . . weird as it sounds, I love who I have become without you. Our life together was very good. And with each passing day through His gentle leading, the Lord is teaching me that my life after your death, although different from all of my dreams and plans, can be just as beautiful and just as good. He truly does bring beauty from ashes.

I miss you. I love you so very much. Still.

I'll see ya later . . .

Dear Family and Friends,

Thank you so much for your continued prayer and love for my family as we have lived these long days of our lives without Tom. We are truly blessed to be so loved by each of you. Thank you for letting us be who we are; for not expecting us to change the pattern of our lives or what is behind the "happy face" that we sometimes wear. Knowing that often it's just a facade that helps us make it through to the next day. Having the freedom to be ourselves, knowing that we are loved and accepted just as we are is a refreshing and wonderful gift. Your kind, encouraging words and the memories of Tom you have shared with us over the years have been a soothing balm for our tender hearts. My children and I are blessed beyond what we deserve to call you our family and friends.

Dear Kitty,

I was five years old when our families met, and for the last fifty=one years you have impacted my life for the Lord. You've been a living example of how to graciously walk through life's celebrations and triumphs as well as the unexpected trials and times of deep sadness . . . all with a joyful heart. Just like the little songbird, you are always singing or humming a lovely tune. You are not only my husband's mom, my children's grammy, and my mother-in-law . . . you are my dear friend. You love me big and without reservation. You love me well. I am blessed that I was chosen by God to be a part of your family. I love you!

Dear Momma and Daddy,

You taught me all that I know about love, marriage, commitment, contentment, faith, and family relationships. Your consistent walk with the Lord and your faithfulness to pray for me and each of my children by name every day is a source of strength to me. Your selfless investment in my life has made me who I am today. During your sixty years together, you've buried your parents, a son-in-law, siblings, and close friends. You've stood in the gap for others whose marriages and homes were crumbling, often picking up the pieces and helping the wounded start over, joyfully giving from your bounty, and joyfully giving when you have been in need. You raised two children, and now your little family of four has grown to eighteen with others who are considered children and grandchildren. You opened your home to many of our friends whose home life was not a secure and loving place to be. Without apology, you live what you taught us, that the real blessing comes in the giving not in the receiving. You are simply the very best, and I am so proud and honored to be your daughter.

I love you and I'm crazy about you!

Dear April, Ali, Amy, and Andrew,

I am convinced that despite how the world will try to spin our story as something tragic and disastrous, God is working something beautiful in each of our lives. Sometimes the pain and the memories are too raw and it's hard to imagine the miracle the He has in store for us. But if we keep trusting in His goodness, He will not leave us in our brokenness. He will restore our lives. He will restore our hearts.

Thank you for your belief in me and your encouragement to step out in faith and trust God's plan for my life. That you belong to me is one of my greatest blessings. You are my dream come true, and I love you so much more than you can ever know.

—Momma

"In your unfailing love, you will lead the people you have redeemed" *(Exodus 15:13).*

CPSIA information can be obtained
at www.ICGtesting.com
Printed in the USA
BVHW07s2025151018
530243BV00001B/7/P